ELIE WIESEL

From the Kingdom of Memory

REMINISCENCES

SUMMIT BOOKS

NEW YORK · LONDON · TORONTO
TOKYO · SYDNEY · SINGAPORE

SUMMIT BOOKS
Simon & Schuster Building
Rockefeller Center
1230 Avenue of the Americas
New York, New York 10020

Copyright © 1990 by Elirion Associates, Inc.
All rights reserved
including the right of reproduction
in whole or in part in any form.
SUMMIT BOOKS *and colophon are*
trademarks of Simon & Schuster Inc.
Designed by Edith Fowler
Manufactured in the United States of America

10 9 8 7 6 5 4 3 2 1

Library of Congress Cataloging in Publication Data

Wiesel, Elie.
  From the kingdom of memory : reminiscences /
Elie Wiesel.
     p. cm.
   1. Wiesel, Elie, 1928– —Political and social
views. 2. Civilization, Modern—20th century.
3. Human rights. 4. Peace. I. Title.
PQ2683.I32Z464 1990
815'.54—dc20   90–9631
ISBN 0–671–52332–5   CIP

See page 251 for Acknowledgments.

FOR ELISHA, AGAIN

CONTENTS

PREFACE

If there is a single theme that dominates all my writings, all my obsessions, it is that of memory—because I fear forgetfulness as much as hatred and death. To forget is, for a Jew, to deny his people—and all that it symbolizes—and also to deny himself. Hence my desire to forget neither where I come from, nor what influenced my choices: the haunted sites of my childhood; the land of malediction where in an instant youngsters grew old; the people I met along the way.

Remember . . . Remember that you were a slave in Egypt. Remember to sanctify the Sabbath . . . Remember Amalek, who wanted to annihilate you . . . No other Biblical Commandment is as persistent. Jews live and grow under the sign of memory. "Do not forget that you are Jewish," are the words—perhaps the last—Jewish parents used to say to their sons and daughters when they left home. To be Jewish is to remember—to claim our right to memory as well as our duty to keep it alive.

Through the recent past I find my distant origins, going back to Moses and Abraham. It is in their name too that I communicate my quest. When a Jew prays, he links his prayer to those of David and the Besht. When a Jew despairs, it is Jeremiah's sadness that makes him weep. The Jew's memory draws its strength from that of his people, and beyond it, from humankind.

For memory is a blessing: it creates bonds rather than destroys them. Bonds between present and past, between individuals and groups. It is because I remember our common beginning that I move closer to my fellow human beings. It is because I refuse to forget that their future is as important as my own. What would the future of man be if it were devoid of memory?

*From
the Kingdom
of Memory*

Why I Write

WHY DO I WRITE? Perhaps in order not to go mad. Or, on the contrary, to touch the bottom of madness.

Like Samuel Beckett, the survivor expresses himself *en désespoir de cause*, because there is no other way.

Speaking of the solitude of the survivor, the great Yiddish and Hebrew poet and thinker Aaron Zeitlin addresses those who have left him: his dead father, his dead brother, his dead friends. "You have abandoned me," he says to them. "You are together, without me. I am here. Alone. And I make words."

So do I, just like him. I too speak words, write words, reluctantly.

There are easier occupations, far more pleasant ones. For the survivor, however, writing is not a profession, but a calling; "an honor," according to Camus. As he put it: "I entered literature through worship." Other writers have said, "Through anger; through love." As for myself, I would say, "Through silence."

It was by seeking, by probing silence that I began to discover the perils and power of the word.

I never intended to be a novelist. The only role I sought was that of witness. I believed that, having survived by chance, I was duty-bound to give meaning to my survival, to justify each moment of my life. I knew the story had to be told. Not to transmit an experience is to betray it; this is what Jewish tradition teaches us. But how to do this?

"When Israel is in exile, so is the word," says the *Book of Splendor*. The word has deserted the meaning it was intended to convey—one can no longer make them coincide. The displacement, the shift, is irrevocable. This was never more true than right after the upheaval. We all knew that we could never say what had to be said, that we could never express in words— coherent, intelligible words—our experience of madness on an absolute scale. The walk through fiery nights, the silence before and after the selection, the toneless praying of the condemned, the Kaddish of the dying, the fear and hunger of the sick, the shame and suffering, the haunted eyes, the wild stares—I thought that I would never be able to speak of them. All words seemed inadequate, worn, foolish, lifeless, whereas I wanted them to sear.

Where was I to discover a fresh vocabulary, a primeval language? The language of night was not human; it was primitive, almost animal—hoarse shouting, screaming, muffled moaning, savage howling, the sounds of beating. . . . A brute strikes wildly, a body falls; an officer raises his arm and a whole community walks toward a common grave; a soldier shrugs his shoulders and a thousand families are torn apart, to be reunited only by death. Such was the language of the concentration camp. It negated all other language and took its place. Rather than link people, it became a wall between them. Could the wall be scaled? Could the reader be brought to the other side? I knew the answer to be No, and yet I also knew that No had to become Yes. This was the wish, the last will of the dead. One had to shatter the wall encasing the darkest truth, and give it a name. One had to force man to look.

The fear of forgetting: the main obsession of all those who have passed through the universe of the damned. The enemy relied on people's disbelief and forgetfulness.

Remember, said the father to his son, and the son to his friend: gather the names, the faces, the tears. If, by a miracle, you come out of it alive, try to reveal everything, omitting nothing, forgetting nothing. Such was the oath we had all taken: "If, by some miracle, I survive, I will devote my life to testifying on behalf of all those whose shadows will be bound to mine forever."

This is why I write certain things rather than others: to remain faithful.

Of course, there are times of doubt for the survivor, times when one gives in to weakness, or longs for comfort. I hear a voice within me telling me to stop mourning the past. I too want to sing of love and its magic. I too want to celebrate the sun, and the dawn that heralds the sun. I would like to shout, and shout loudly: "Listen, listen well! I too am capable of victory, do you hear? I too am open to laughter and joy. I want to walk head high, my face unguarded." One feels like shouting, but the shout becomes a murmur. One must make a choice; one must remain faithful. This is what the survivor feels; he owes nothing to the living, but everything to the dead.

I owe the dead my memory. I am duty-bound to serve as their emissary, transmitting the history of their disappearance, even if it disturbs, even if it brings pain. Not to do so would be to betray them, and thus myself. I simply look at them. I see them and I write.

While writing, I question them as I question myself. I write to understand as much as to be understood. Will I succeed one day? Wherever one starts from, one reaches darkness. God? He remains the God of darkness. Man? The source of darkness. The killers' sneers, their victims' tears, the onlookers' indifference, their complicity and complacency: I do not understand the divine role in all that. A million children massacred: I will never understand.

Jewish children: they haunt my writings. I see them again and again. I shall always see them. Hounded, humiliated, bent like the old men who surround them trying to protect them, in vain. They are thirsty, the children, and there is no one to give them water. They are hungry, the children, but there is no one to give them a crust of bread. They are afraid, and there is no one to reassure them.

They walk in the middle of the road, like urchins. They are on the way to the station, and they will never return. In sealed cars, without air or food, they travel toward another world; they guess where they are going, they know it, and they keep silent. They listen to the wind, the call of death in the distance.

All these children, these old people, I see them. I never stop seeing them. I belong to them.

But they, to whom do they belong?

People imagine that a murderer weakens when facing a child. That the child might reawaken the killer's lost humanity. That the killer might be unable to kill the child before him.

Not this time. With us, it happened differently. Our Jewish children had no effect upon the killers. Nor upon the world. Nor upon God.

I think of them, I think of their childhood. Their childhood in a small Jewish town, and this town is no more. They frighten me; they reflect an image of myself, one that I pursue and run from at the same time— the image of a Jewish adolescent who knew no fear except the fear of God, whose faith was whole, comforting.

No, I do not understand. And if I write, it is to warn the reader that he will not understand either. "You will not understand, you will never understand," were the words heard everywhere in the kingdom of night. I can only echo them.

An admission of impotence and guilt? I do not know. All I know is that Treblinka and Auschwitz cannot be told. And yet I have tried. God knows I have tried.

Did I attempt too much, or not enough? Out of some thirty volumes, only three or four try to penetrate the realm of the dead. In my other books, through my other books, I try to follow other roads. For it is dangerous to linger among the dead; they hold on to you, and you run the risk of speaking only to them. And so, I forced myself to turn away from them and study other periods, explore other destinies and teach other tales: the Bible and the Talmud, Hasidism and its fervor, the *shtetl* and its songs, Jerusalem and its echoes; the Russian Jews and their anguish, their awakening, their courage. At times it seems to me that I am speaking of other things with the sole purpose of keeping the essential—the personal experience—unspoken. At times I wonder: And what if I was wrong? Perhaps I should have stayed in my own world with the dead.

But then, the dead never leave me. They have their rightful place even in the works about pre-Holo-

caust Hasidism or ancient Jerusalem. Even in my
Biblical and Midrashic tales, I pursue their presence,
mute and motionless. The presence of the dead then
beckons so forcefully that it touches even the most removed characters. Thus, they appear on Mount Moriah, where Abraham is about to sacrifice his son, a
Holocaust offering to their common God. They appear
on Mount Nebo, where Moses confronts solitude and
death. And again in the *Pardess*, the orchard of secret
knowledge, where a certain Elisha ben Abuya, seething
with anger and pain, decides to repudiate his faith.
They appear in Hasidic and Talmudic legends in
which victims forever need defending against forces
that would crush them. Technically, so to speak, they
are of course elsewhere, in time and space, but on a
deeper, truer plane, the dead are part of every story, of
every scene. They die with Isaac, lament with Jeremiah, they sing with the Besht and, like him, wait for
miracles—but alas, they will not come to pass.

"But what is the connection?" you will ask. Believe me, there is one. After Auschwitz everything long
past brings us back to Auschwitz. When I speak of
Abraham, Isaac, and Jacob, when I evoke Rabbi Yohanan ben Zakkai and Rabbi Akiba, it is the better to
understand them in the light of Auschwitz. As for the
Maggid of Mezeritch and his disciples, it is to encounter the followers of their followers that I attempt to
reconstruct their spellbinding universe. I like to imagine them alive, exuberant, celebrating life and hope.

Their happiness is as necessary to me as it once was to themselves. And yet . . .

How did they manage to keep their faith intact? How did they manage to sing as they went to meet the Angel of Death? I know Hasidim who never wavered in their faith; I respect their strength. I know others who chose rebellion, protest, rage; I respect their courage. For there comes a time when only those who do believe in God will cry out to him in wrath and anguish. The faith of some matters as much as the strength of others. It is not ours to judge; it is only ours to tell the tale.

But where is one to begin? Whom is one to include? One meets a Hasid in all my novels. And a child. And an old man. And a beggar. And a madman. They are all part of my inner landscape. Why? They are pursued and persecuted by the killers; I offer them shelter. The enemy wanted to create a society purged of their presence, and I have brought some of them back. The world denied them, repudiated them: so let them live at least within the feverish dreams of my characters.

It is for them that I write.

And yet, the survivor may experience remorse. He has tried to bear witness; it was all in vain.

After the liberation, illusions shaped our hopes. We were convinced that a new world would be built upon the ruins of Europe. A new civilization would dawn. No more wars, no more hate, no more intolerance, no fanaticism anywhere. And all this because the witnesses would speak, and speak they did. Was it to no avail?

They will continue, for they cannot do otherwise. When man, in his grief, falls silent, Goethe says, then God gives him the strength to sing of his sorrows. From that moment on, he may no longer choose not to sing, whether his song is heard or not. What matters is to struggle against silence with words, or through another form of silence. What matters is to gather a smile here and there, a tear here and there, a word here and there, and thus justify the faith placed in man, a long time ago, by so many victims.

Why do I write? To wrest those victims from oblivion. To help the dead vanquish death.

To Believe
or Not to Believe

SOMEWHERE in the Carpathian Mountains, at the other end of my life, a Jewish child is saying his daily prayers. He closes his eyes to concentrate better, swaying to and fro as if to break out of the rhythm of his daily pursuits. Just before concluding, he repeats the Thirteen Principles of Faith exactly as a certain physician from Cordoba, the great philosopher and codifier Moses Maimonides, the Rambam, formulated them eight centuries earlier—clear and immutable principles which serve to buttress all who need them.

"I believe with perfect faith that the Creator, Blessed be His name, is the author and guide of everything that has been created . . . I believe that the Creator is the first and last . . . He rewards those who keep His Commandments and punishes those who transgress against them . . . The Torah will not be changed and there never will be any other Law . . . I believe in the coming of the Messiah, and, though he may tarry, I will wait daily for his coming. . . ."

I look at that Jewish child who prays and is afraid to look; I listen and envy him.

For him, for me, it was once so simple. I feared God while loving him. I came to terms with exile while regretting it. I loved my parents and admired my teachers. I was a believer, as they say. And if I questioned my belief at all, it was only for fear that it might not be sufficiently perfect.

As for my place in an uncertain world, my aim in an ephemeral life—I had no doubts on that score. It was up to man, as God's creation, to make the universe more welcoming. To bring redemption closer. Wasn't this inordinately ambitious? So what? For us, in the Diaspora, being a Jew meant bridging the summit and the abyss, reconciling the worst torment with the most sublime hope. Imprisoned up there in divine time, the Messiah could expect deliverance from none other than man, below. Although a work of God, the Torah is not within God's grasp: those who study it, and they alone, are qualified to interpret the Law. Do these seem dangerous paradoxes? For us, life itself was a paradox, and danger did not frighten us.

In those days I simply could not conceive of a Jew who did not define himself through his faith. Jews had the choice: loyalty or denial. A faithless Jew was a renegade, outlawed from the community of Israel, therefore despicable. And dangerous. I had read enough on the subject to know how much distress was caused by renegades; they were to be found at more than one crossroad of Jewish suffering.

If you had asked any Jewish mother, from the Dnieper to the Vistula, what she most wished for her children, she would invariably have replied: "All I want is that they grow up to be good Jews." What, precisely, did being a good Jew mean? It meant taking upon oneself the entire destiny of the Jewish people; it meant living in more than one period, listening to more than one discourse, being part of more than one system; it meant accepting the teachings of Hillel as well as of Shamai, and following Rabbi Akiba no less passionately than one followed his adversary, Rabbi Ishmael; it meant summoning joy on festive days and retreating into sadness when in mourning; it meant being ready to sacrifice oneself to sanctify the Name without even being sure that the Name desired the sacrifice, or that it was not He who conferred upon the executioner his might, if not his right. . . .

For the child I was, that last question did not arise. I was convinced that everything emanated from God. If He punished us, He had a reason: All we had to do was trust in Him and thank Him. Who was I to dare to chart the paths of heaven? I was obliged to

choose between good and evil but not to define what
they were: their definition was the province of the Supreme Judge. It was often through chastisement that
He showed us the significance and consequences of
our actions; we may have thought we were doing good
while we committed evil. Was this process unjust? It is
a good question, but one which brooks no answer.

A Talmudic legend: Moses, impressed by Rabbi
Akiba's erudition, wanted to know what would happen
to him. God showed him the tragic end of the great
master who, in a market square in occupied Judea, suffered the torture the Romans reserved for rebels.
Moses cried out: "O Lord, is this Thy justice? Is this
the reward for having studied Thy Law?" And God
replied: "Be silent, you cannot understand."

Moses was silent. But my teachers asked: "What
was good enough for Moses is not good enough for
you?" I was obliged to respond that, in effect, it was
sufficient for those who believed in Moses. "For a
believer," said a Hasidic rabbi, "there are no questions; for an unbeliever there are no answers."

All this seemed irrefutable, then. And today? I
have written and I have spoken but have I said all I
wanted to say? Have I learned to distinguish between
the essential and the frivolous? What is the meaning
of history? What is the future of mankind? I have a
son, I have students. Why should they be responsible
for a world they did not create? In the name of what
belief shall I attempt to inculcate on them the no-

tions and precepts which were taught me when I was their age?

Before emphasizing what I believe, perhaps I should point out what I do not believe, or what I no longer believe: I no longer believe in the magic of the spoken word. It signifies not order but disorder. It does not eliminate chaos, it only conceals it. It no longer carries men's hopes but distorts them. It has ceased to be a vehicle, only to become an obstacle. It does not signify sharing but compromise.

Yet, through my tradition, and also my vocation, my relationship with language was a solemn celebration. Indispensable to the development of man, language is his ultimate expression; there were those who attributed mystical powers to speech. Life and death are dependent on the tongue, according to Ecclesiastes. The destiny of the world depends on it. The name of the Messiah precedes the Messiah. The spoken word preceded creation itself. Because of that word, the world emerged from nothingness and light parted from the dark. Before acting, God spoke. Language introduced mankind into history, not the reverse.

Jewish youngsters knew the lullaby *Oif'n pripitchik*, which women in the ghettos sang to their children. It tells of a rabbi who is teaching his small pupils the *aleph-bet*: "When you grow up, you will come to understand how much pain and how many tears these letters contain." And joy. And majesty.

The Midrash describes how Moses, pleading for

his people, called on the letters of the alphabet as witnesses for the defense: "My people have done enough for you, now it is your turn to show your gratitude." The Bible and its commentaries, the Talmud and its interpretations—the infinite indeed exists and is to be found in words, words which sooner or later will be made to explode. A strange, primal, unique light traverses them and causes them to vibrate with life and truth. The Baal Shem Tov, it is said, used to read the *Zohar* while his eyes surveyed the earth from end to end; we Jewish children would listen to this legend and, in our imagination, we would see the rabbi stopping to smile at us and show us the way.

Few other ancient cultures or living civilizations are so imbued with a passion for words. As the Hasidic tradition has it, it was not the Ark that saved Noah—but eloquence. In Hebrew, *teva* denotes both "ark" and "letter." In order to save him from the Flood, God commanded Noah to construct a language which would serve as both shelter and refuge. When they were driven out of their country by the Babylonians, and then by the Romans, the Jewish people took with them only a few laws, some memories and various customs consigned to a book, but this book enabled them to resist temptation and defeat danger. Thanks to the Talmud, they could continue to inhabit Jerusalem from afar. Murderers might be sharpening their knives in the marketplace outside, but in the house of prayer and study just a few steps away, the sages and their disciples would be engaged in a debate that began a thousand years before. Linked to David's kingdom by the language of memory, the exiles kept it alive by featuring it in their stories and praying for it to be rebuilt. The third Temple, says a Midrashic text, will be indestructibly fashioned of fire; we preferred to think that words would contain the fire.

The martyrdom of the great Rabbi Hanania ben Teradyon is beautifully told in a Talmudic legend. The Romans, having condemned the rabbi to perish at the stake for teaching the Torah in public, wrapped him in the sacred scrolls and set them afire. His disciples asked him, "Master, what do you see?" He told them: "I see the parchment burning but the letters are floating in the air." For the letters cannot be destroyed; the enemy will always be rendered impotent by the power of language.

This legend is part of the liturgy of Yom Kippur, but it is valid every day of the year. It describes how a Jew felt whenever he was persecuted. "Our enemy may kill us but he is powerless against what we embody."

"Lord," declared Rabbi Levi Yitzhak of Berdichev, "I want to strike a bargain with you. I would like to compose the eulogies and litanies you deserve but as I am no poet let me give you the twenty-two letters of your sacred tongue: you will make better use of them than I."

For some part of every word is sacred; all words should lean toward the sacred. Today we are articulating words which Yitzhak and Jeremiah uttered under other skies and in other contexts. If our words sound different, that is our fault; we forget that God is listening.

The children of Israel were rescued in Egypt, according to the Talmud, because they remained true to their language. If King David were to return to his city, he would be able to understand what its inhabitants are saying to one another; better still: they would understand him. The words of the Lord heard at Sinai still retain their full authority and freshness today.

Our own words are no more than a vehicle reflecting the divine communication. That is their justification. But does all this amount to excessive respect for human speech? It is language that connects us to the mystery of the beginning and, at the same time, to that of survival. God, at Sinai, uttered just one word, *Anochi*, I, but that word contained all the words which man, from the beginning, and till the end of time, will have spoken, whether to spread His glory or to bring His curse upon himself.

Nowadays, man speaks loudly and volubly. There has never been so much talk. Television, radio, satellite telecommunications, speeches, interviews, commentaries, news analyses: modern man is bombarded with so many voices that he no longer hears any. Least of all his own.

Might that be because of his fear of being overtaken by events? Might man be afraid of not being able to express himself in time?

All this applies equally to writing. It seems there has never been so much of it. And definitely never so much in print. Was Ecclesiastes right to include literary inflation among the eschatalogical maledictions?

There was a time when a book, any book, aroused in me a feeling of reverence. I would stroke it, sniff it before opening it. If the volume was in Hebrew and dealt with religious matters, I would kiss it before closing it. If it chanced to slip and drop to the floor, I would rush to pick it up and ask its forgiveness.

Today it's different. Mystics speak of "the exile of language." Like the *Shekinah*, Divine Presence, language has followed Israel into exile. What does exiled language mean? It refers to the distance between words and what they mask. It signifies the tension between language and its subject.

This phenomenon is not restricted to one language or one society; it is virtually universal. In every modern country one witnesses this verbal inflation, and a resulting devaluation of words. Political parties "war" with each other, industrial enterprises launch "offensives," critics "massacre" novels or plays, journalists praise or condemn the latest "revolution" in *haute couture*. On another plane, Stalin built the Gulag to "re-educate" his citizens and Lavrenty Beria (Soviet Intelligence chief during Stalin's regime) annihilated hundreds of thousands of people for the "salvation" of humanity; as for Hitler, he invented the terms "concentration camp" and "final solution," and all for the "well-being" of the human race.

Hitler distorted language as never before. Neither Emperor Nero nor Attila the Hun concealed their crimes with grandiloquent phrases. The Inquisition called its tortures and executions by name. Marat and Robespierre did not seek a pleasant-sounding euphemism to justify the Terror. Until the Nazi reign, killers killed and said so; torturers tortured and were proud of it. But the Nazis assassinated thousands upon thousands of Jews and spoke of "special treatment." "Things, objects," meant human beings. "Relocation" signified deportation, evacuation, liquidation: extermination. Night and fog are evocative words; we now know what they hid. Similarly, the word "selection." Thanks to this verbal technique, the assassins succeeded in convincing themselves that they were not assassins. By "obeying," they were doing no more than "purifying" Europe of its Jews.

There are certain German words I can no longer use, said Nobel Prize-winning German-Jewish poet Nelly Sachs when I visited her in Stockholm.

Have I myself written too much about the camps? Some of my colleagues tell me so. If only, they say, you could speak about something else. As a matter of fact, I do. I write on ancient themes from the Bible and the

Talmud, and on the Hasidic world, Jerusalem, and Russian Jews in order to free myself from the theme which seems to me the most consuming, the most urgent of all. One day I, too, would like to compose a novel in which the landscape is not reduced to ashes; one day I, too, would like to sing of life and celebrate love. But not yet. . . .

In one of my novels, a character is shot at point-blank range but he cannot die: all his family are dead, all his friends are dead, he is the last one left, and because he is the last he is unable to die; but his killer says to him, "One day you will curse me for having spared you, even if I didn't intend to; you will speak but no one will listen; you will tell the truth but it will be the truth of a madman."

All survivors are a bit like that: our memories are those of madmen. How can we get the doors to open? What can we do to share our visions? Our words can only evoke the incomprehensible. Hunger, thirst, fear, humiliation, waiting, death; for us these words hold different realities. This is the ultimate tragedy of the victims.

What we suffered has no place within language: it is somewhere beyond life and history. The ghetto and the sealed cars, the children hurled alive into the flames, the dumb old men with slit throats, the mothers with crazed eyes, the sons powerless to relieve their fathers' agony: a "normal" person cannot take in so much horror. A normal person cannot absorb so much darkness, nor can he understand, or ever hope to understand.

Here lies the tragedy of the witness: What shall he do with his testimony? He incessantly asks himself the meaning of a survival some mistakenly call miraculous; he feels guilty toward the dead who have charged him with an impossible mission; he is destined to feel that he exists in the place of someone else.

Formerly, thoughts became experiences and experiences became words, but today this process is interrupted. Today we must admit that certain experiences defy language. Speech is no longer the logical result. And all the discourse on the "lessons" of Auschwitz and the "message" of Treblinka—lessons about ethics and politics, messages to do with theology—have nothing at all to do with the experience of Night.

The morning after the storm, facing a horrified world, the survivors of the camps could only repeat, "You cannot understand, you cannot understand." Later, invariably for humanitarian reasons, they tried to explain. After all, people had to be made aware, warned of certain dangers, shown the paths it was perilous to take. Yet each time the witnesses had to suffer anew in order to reveal themselves even partially, in order to speak even haltingly of the most intimate things—is there anything more intimate than pain or death?—and each time, it was a lost cause. The listener either failed to understand or missed the point.

But in that case, you will ask, how should we read all those books, all the novels, accounts, studies? Haven't they so much as lifted the veil? Pointed out the wounds? Indicated the graveyard? Naturally, witnesses must write and readers must read. And yet, I know that their secret cannot really be transmitted.

I do not utter these words without discomfort, without sadness. But I must say them.

The Kabbala speaks of *shvirat hakelim*, the "breaking of vessels" at the moment of creation. In the same way, today we would do well to envisage the possibility of a similar break, on a scale no less vast than the first, involving the totality of being: a break between past and future, between creation and creator, between man and his fellow man.

But then, you will say, what is left? Is there hope despite everything, despite ourselves? Despair, perhaps? Or faith?

All that is left is the question.

Inside a Library

In HIS "Society and Solitude," Emerson said with typical simplicity:

> Consider what you have in the smallest chosen library. A company of the wisest and wittiest men that could be picked out of all civil countries, in a thousand years, have set in best order the results of their learning and wisdom. The men themselves were hidden and inaccessible, solitary, impatient of interruption, fenced by etiquette; but the thought which they did not uncover to their bosom friend is here written out in transparent words to us, the strangers of another age. . . .

True—but what about the books written by fools, literary technicians or fame-hungry authors who have nothing to say—and say it?

Of them, King Solomon said in his Ecclesiastes that their books will be the ultimate malediction: "Of the making of books there will be no end. . . ." Why should this be a curse? Solomon was wise—the wisest of all kings. He knew. He knew that there would be a time when more books would be published than written.

If the school is a temple, then the library is its sanctuary. In the classroom you teach, you learn, you argue; in the library you remain quiet. You read alone; you listen alone. And all of a sudden you discover that you are not alone; you are in the presence of masters and disciples of centuries past; and you grow silent. In the library you are always silent. Not only because you do not want to disturb your fellow students or teachers, but also because you do not raise your voice in a sanctuary: with Rabbi Akiba and Rabbi Shimon ben Yohai present, with the Ari Hakadosh and Rabbi Shneur Zalmen ben Baruch of Ladi in the room, you dare not speak except in a whisper.

That is why I have always felt such deep attachment to libraries. Here, within these walls, there is peace. The old quarrels subside. Maimonides no longer fears the arrows of the Raavid. The Rabbanites and the Karaites live side by side in harmony. The Gaon of Vilna and the Maggid of Mezeritch coexist in peace. All these writers and teachers, all these thinkers and lawmakers who engaged in disputations during their lifetime, now accept one another's views with tolerance and serenity. Because of the books? Because of the silence. Here, words and silence are not in conflict—quite the contrary: they complete and enrich one another. Is it possible? In our tradition—it is.

When the Torah was given at Sinai, says Rabbi Abahu in the name of Rabbi Yohanan, the birds did not chirp, the beasts did not growl, the sea did not roar, and the wind did not stir: the entire universe was silent. And then, when God spoke and said *Anochi*, "I," the words entered silence without breaking it.

There lies the beauty and the enchantment of the library: within its walls, everything is possible.

But then—what is a library? Simply a room with bookshelves? The answer may disappoint some of you but it is Yes: any room with books and students can turn into a library—just as any home can become a house of study and prayer. Isn't this the teaching we received from Rabbi Yohanan ben Zakkai? Wherever Jews gather to study Torah, the *Shekinah* dwells among them. Erected by man for God, the Temple does not imprison Him; quite the contrary, it frees Him and calls Him to join His creation. Thus every home becomes a sanctuary, every table is transformed into an altar, and every person performs the functions of the High Priest.

And so, any room can become a library; only, once it has been a library, it can never again be a simple room.

There are secret corners, hidden words in a library. A few words on the margin of a page. Dates of birth and death on the inside covers of prayer books. Tears, invisible but real, shed by a grandmother who wished to be heard by God—at least by God. Occasionally, you will discover a tale which encompasses another tale, a name which conceals another story.

Look there: the *Valley of Tears*, by Rabbi Mordechai Yoseph Hacohen of Avignon. Avignon occupies a special place in Jewish history—*and* literature. Jews lived there in peace, while around them Jewish blood was shed.

I never saw my grandfather without a book in his hands. Occasionally, when he was tired, he would doze off for a minute or an hour—but he continued, in his sleep, to chant the passage he was studying. . . .

My father had books in his grocery store. While waiting for customers, he would open one and read—and smile. I shall never forget his smile.

He was not alone in living with such passion for books; most Jews in my town, and in all Jewish towns, shared that passion. Idleness was the greatest of sins. You have nothing to *do?* a father would admonish his son: take a book—any book. You prayed *minchah* too early, you had to wait for *maariv?* Take a book. You have a headache? The Talmud offers you the best and cheapest remedy: study—and you will feel better. You cannot study? You are unable to understand Talmud or Zohar? Study Chumash and its accessible commentaries. Read the work of Rabbi Chaim ben Atar—the friend of the Besht who waited for him in Jerusalem. Had they met, says Hasidic legend, the Messiah would have appeared to save his people—and all others. You are unable to study the Bible? Say Psalms. You could hardly find a Jew in the *shtetl* who did not possess a prayer book with Psalms.

As a child, I would spend my meager allowance on books . . . I remember the bookstores and their owners: Rabbi Avigdor Greenwald, whose brother was a rabbi in Cincinnati, and Reb Shlomo Weiss. I would buy more books than I could afford, but my credit was good . . . I did not deserve it. Many books were left unpaid—but it was not my fault. A certain event occurred and our lives were interrupted. When I left for that place, I had in my knapsack more books than food.

Strange: when I returned to my hometown, many years later, I found some of my cherished volumes, lying in dust together with thousands and thousands of books, in the Wizhnitzer House of Study, where I had spent days and nights learning and praying—and waiting for the coming of the Messiah.

May I offer a suggestion? Redeem those books— and all the others that are waiting to be redeemed in all the formerly Jewish towns and hamlets. Send students to locate them, collect them—and bring them back to Israel and the Jewish people, the Jewish pupils, to whom they belong. It would help the students— for they would learn much about Eastern European Jewry, its glory and tragedy—and it would help the books. Those that students would find in my town alone would be sufficient to fill a library.

They will read, and their reading will become one more adventure—a source of excitement and wonder. And anguish too. One never knows what to expect in the next line, on the next page: another catastrophe? another warning? another miracle? To read means to open gates and go back to ancient times—and bring back ancient experiences.

My teachers taught me to question the text. To decipher it. To examine it from all angles, to peal away appearances and go to the essence—to the original meaning—but not straight away: one had to learn the superimposed structures as well. So when I would come home, my mother would not ask me whether I made an interesting discovery but, on the contrary, whether I had asked a good question.

The Jewish tradition of learning—*is* learning. Adam chose knowledge instead of immortality. If our forefather is Abraham and not Noah, it is because Abraham shared his knowledge with others, whereas Noah did not. When Jacob felt he was about to die, he blessed his children—and his blessings were teachings. Moses's greatness? He could have kept the Law to himself but did not. Every Jewish person is commanded to write down every word of the poetry in the Torah, and thus transmit it.

The most urgent commandment? A father must educate his children. He himself must do it, and not rely on Sunday school teachers.

I remember the first day I went to *cheder*, the first lesson in Chumash, the first obstacles I had to surmount in the Talmud. I remember the voice of my first teacher who taught me the alphabet; I remember his sadness when I read poorly. I remember my master who opened the gates of Talmud and the gates of the Zohar for me. Why has God used words as instruments of creation? Because all of creation lies in them. All of creation could be destroyed by them. And redeemed again.

Commentaries on the Bible, on the commentaries themselves; Hasidic tales of wonder and fear: I remember where I sat, what I did, what I felt when I discovered them. I also remember my first—and premature—encounter with apocrypha—with forbidden knowledge.

One *Shabbat* afternoon, in the house of study, I found a book which somebody must have hidden on the top shelf. I opened it: it was a book of commentaries on the Bible by a certain Reb Moshe Dessauer, better known as Moses Mendelssohn. An old Hasid looked at the book in my hands. What are you reading? he asked. When he saw the name, he took it away and gave me a slap in the face that hurts me to this very day.

LEARNING IS PART of Judaism—and Judaism means learning. This is a command that all must follow—God included. The Talmud—and the Zohar—are full of stories about the Almighty teaching a course somewhere in heaven, with the *tzaddikim* as his disciples. Paradise? A great Yeshiva. What else? In our collective fantasy, the Yeshiva epitomized all sacred ambitions and lofty desires. When a Biblical—or Talmudic—hero disappeared, and we didn't know where, we imagined him in a Yeshiva. When Abraham left Mount Moriah alone, where did Isaac go? To a Yeshiva. The best thing that could happen to a person was to enter a good Yeshiva—and find a good master—and learn a good page of Talmud. Torah therefore doesn't mean only *mitzvot*, good deeds, but also the study of the *mitzvot*. And the Torah of Israel doesn't mean the religion of Israel, but the study and the teaching of Israel. Hence the passion a Jew has for the Torah—it is physical. The way he holds the Torah. And kisses it. And clings to it: pure passion.

During—and after—each catastrophe, Jews wanted to know its meaning, its implications, its scope, its roots, and its place in history—or in God's vision of history. Thus every disaster was followed by a surge of study, prayer, mystical quest, meditation, or scholarly endeavor. The reading of the Torah was established by Ezra and Nehemiah after the first destruction of the Temple—after Babylonian exile became reality. The Talmud was preceded by the second destruction of the Temple. The Crusades moved our people to messianic experiments—as did the pogroms, though on different levels and under different guises. Collective pain produced works of contemplation, poetry, and philosophy. Why? We felt the need to understand. To turn experience into knowledge—and then, only then, knowledge into experience. Why should pagans say, "Where is your God?" was a question we used to address to God as well as to ourselves. Why, why are we to be singled out, always, for all woes? Why are we in a situation which allows other nations to mock us, ridicule us, saying, Where is the Jewish God? Out of so many questions, many hypotheses—if not many answers—were formulated. Mostly religious ones, involving the age-old concept of sin and punishment: we suffer because we have sinned. There was—there is—a logic in our trials. Why were we sent into exile? Because we have sinned. But then—if we have sinned, we should be humble. We were not; strangely we took credit for our very punishment. God punishes only those He loves, we were told. He must have loved us very much. And we were right in feeling pride. Not for having suffered, but for having felt the need, for having had the strength, to explore the history of that suffering: for having managed to understand it—thus disarm and even conquer it. For having had the obsession to record that history in books.

When I travel, I am always afraid of running out of books. Half of my luggage consists of reading material and the other half of writing material.

If I had to describe hell, it would be as a place without books. What would life be without their appeal to our fantasy, without their power to change things simply by revealing their hidden message.

Both Hitler and Stalin understood the importance of books for the Jew. That is why they burned them in Germany and destroyed them in Russia. Stalin's police went so far as demolishing the Jewish presses in Moscow, Kiev, and Odessa. His pathological hatred was vented on both the Jewish faith and Jewish culture: the Hebrew or Yiddish alphabet annoyed him, angered him, defied him—that is why he condemned it to death. Except . . . he did not succeed. Like Rabbi Hananya ben Teradyon, we can testify: yes, the parchments may burn, but not the letters—not the spirit—not the vision—not the soul of a people, a people committed to eternal values, and thus to eternity.

And yet, there has been a certain reluctance among some of the masters to write books. The Ari Hakadosh never wrote anything; nor did the Besht; as for Rabbi Nahman, he ordered his faithful scribe Reb Nathan to burn his writings and send them back

to heaven. Rabbi Bunam of Pshiskhe wrote a book en-
titled *The Book of Man;* it was meant to include
everything concerning life and man, history and faith,
past and future—a grandiose project whose stunning
aspect was that the author wanted his book to consist
of one page alone. So every day he wrote that page,
and every evening he burned it.

As for the celebrated solitary visionary of Kotzk,
he once explained why he refused to write books:
Who would read them? he asked. Some villager.
When would he have time to read them? Not during
the week. Only on the Sabbath. In the evening? No,
too tired. In the morning, then? Yes, after services.
After the Sabbath meal. He would take the book—my
book—and lie down on the sofa, ready and willing to
see what I had to say about Torah and Talmud. But
then the man would be so tired that, after glancing at
the first page, he would doze off, dreaming about other
things—and his book, my book, would fall to the floor.
And for him I should write books?

But what about all those books that were not
written? Our history has been preserved elsewhere,
through other methods, too, we know that. In litur-
gical chants we learn more about the life and the lore,
the anguish and the defiance of Jewish communities
than in precisely edited volumes. In the *responsa* we
discover more about the problems that agitated our
brethren throughout centuries, in numerous places,
than in documents. Jewish history may also be deci-

phered on tombstones. On prison walls. Some chapters were written, like the Torah, with fire on fire. Read their descriptions and your sleep will be haunted by their mute despair, and by their determination to overcome despair. Or, in more recent times, read the chronicles from ghettos and death camps: read the *Sonderkommando* documents and your life will be altered.

Eventually, it is with regret that one leaves this place of meditation and memory—one leaves it, having been enriched, enhanced, and yet one does not want to leave it at all.

But then, you do not really leave a library; if you do what it wants you to do, then you are taking it with you.

The Stranger in the Bible

ON THAT NIGHT Abraham had a vision both magnificent and awesome. He heard God renewing His solemn promise that Abraham would not die without an heir. That his passage on earth, his journey among men, would be neither forgotten nor erased. And that the future would justify his past—for mankind would look at the world through his eyes. He, Abraham, would be the first of a line never to be broken, the founder of a nation never to dissolve.

And yet—despite God's soothing, reassuring voice, Abraham hesitated; he wanted to believe but could not, not really, not entirely.

Abraham could not suppress his anxiety: so far God had promised him everything and given him little. How long could Abraham wait? Time was running out. He was almost a hundred years old. Thus, when

God told him not to worry—he began to worry. God said, I shall protect you and reward you. And Abraham answered, Yes—but I am still alone. So once again God revealed his future to him: You *will* have a son, he *will* be your heir—lift up your eyes and behold the sky; your children will be like the stars—innumerable; and eternal will be their splendor.

Strange, but Abraham still was not satisfied; he wanted more. He demanded proof: How shall I know that this land will be mine, stay mine?

God's response is astonishing. He told him to take a calf, a goat, and a ram—all three years old. And a pigeon, and a dove. And prepare them for sacrifice. Abraham obeyed. He cut them into pieces and divided them into two lots, one facing the other. And he waited. And when wild birds of prey arrived and tried to devour the sacrificial offerings, he chased them away. Then the sun set, and Abraham fell asleep, his entire being heavy with anguish. And God said unto him, "Know, Abraham, that your descendants will be treated as strangers in foreign lands; they will be sold into slavery; they will be persecuted, tormented. But it will not last forever. For their oppressors will be punished. So, you see, you may die in peace. . . ."

By then the sun had vanished from the horizon and there was darkness from one end of the world to the other. Suddenly, out of the darkness emerged a smoking furnace and a flaming torch and they passed between the offerings. And God concluded His covenant with Abraham: This land, He said, from the Nile to the Euphrates, will belong to your children and theirs. . . .

Thus ends the description—intense and allegorical—of that most important moment in the destiny of our people. If we are what we are—if we are attached to a past which envelops so many years of yearning and so many centuries of exile—it is because on that fateful night, shrouded in secrecy, God and Abraham concluded a covenant which may be viewed as a prefiguration of all that was to follow—until the end of time.

This passage in Scripture is disquieting, notwithstanding its beauty and meaning; its mystery is enhanced by its imagery. What began as vision ended as theater, deserving our scrutiny.

Biblical commentators have all felt that the text was puzzling on more than one level.

First of all, psychologically, Abraham—at this moment of his life—does not need to be reassured; he has just defeated the mightiest kings in the region; he is respected, feared, and loved as well as powerful and rich.

God said, "Do not worry. I shall protect you." Do not worry? If ever Abraham could live without worry, it is *now*.

Then how does one explain Abraham's sudden insecurity? Did the first believer doubt God's pledge to the point of demanding proof? Did he have to remind God that he had no successor? Didn't God know that?

Also, what is the significance of God's stage directions? The animals, the birds, the smoking furnace, the burning torch—what do they all mean?

And then—when was Abraham awake and when was he asleep? This is not clear in the text. The scene is composed of three parts. It opens with Abraham hearing God's voice in a vision; it develops with God telling him to go out. Out of where? And where to? And it ends with Abraham's anguish—while he is asleep—when God foretells both exile and redemption. Was the covenant only a dream? A hallucination? Did Abraham sleep while God spoke?

More important, why did Abraham accept the terms of the covenant? Why didn't he protest against sending his children into exile? Why did he accept suffering on their behalf? Why were they to become strangers?

The Talmud and Rashi—and countless commentators—felt so disturbed, and so moved, by this striking episode that they had to try to explain it.

One explanation was that Abraham was afraid precisely *because* he had been so victorious—afraid of having exhausted his credit. So God had to restore his self-confidence: Do not worry, this is only the beginning, more rewards will come to you.

Why did Abraham demand proof? Rabbi Hiyya, son of Hanina, said that this demand shows his humility and not his arrogance: he wanted proof that he, Abraham, would be worthy of his future. The sacrifices? A hint of future rituals in the Temple. The darkness? The long night of exile. The smoking furnace and the flaming torch? Symbols of punishment, but also of glory and royalty.

Secular scholars offer their own interpretation. For them, the spectacle is nothing but a reflection of ancient pagan rituals, quite common in that region, vestiges of which survived until the time of Jeremiah.

The text is especially important because here, for the first time, the term "stranger" is used: "And your descendants will be strangers in foreign lands. . . ."

Why is the term "stranger" linked to a promise? Why is it part of a covenant? What kind of promise is it anyway? Furthermore, who is a stranger? What is a stranger? When does someone become a stranger— and for how long? What must he say, do, or feel—or make another feel—to be so called? And then, is he to be fought or befriended?

Man, by definition, is born a stranger: coming from nowhere, he is thrust into an alien world which existed before him—a world which didn't need him. And which will survive him.

A stranger, he goes through life meeting other strangers. His only constant companion? Death. Or God. And neither has a name. Or a face. Are they strangers to him too?

Indeed, no topic, no problem is as urgent to our

generation, haunted by a pervasive feeling of loss, failure, and isolation. Once upon a time, past civilizations were remembered for their temples and works of art, or for their pyramids and idols. Ours may well be remembered for certain words and expressions: uselessness, absurdity, alienation.

Existential philosophers use such terms to illustrate their concept of contemporary man as empty, desperate, and estranged from both the world and himself. According to this view, there is between man and society a wall never to be demolished, between man and his conscience an abyss never to be bridged. He can neither love nor hate—neither help nor be helped. He is not free to define himself as mortal among mortals; he is not free—period. His very existence lies in doubt. Whatever he may do, he will do as a stranger; whatever his hope may be, it will perish with him.

Our generation flirts with madness and death— our own, and not only our own. We try anything— nihilism, mysticism, escapism, violence and antiviolence, solitude and communes—to awaken, to attain a sense of belonging, of sharing, of participating: of being alive. *I want to exist* is the leitmotif in modern literature. *You hear me? I want to exist.* There are so many dead in our past that we sometimes feel that we are among them. So what? Better to belong to the dead than to no one.

Meursault, the stranger in the classic novel by

Camus, kills so as to prove that he is alive. Better to be punished than to be ignored. Thus suicide has become a romantic temptation—a protest against an indifferent society.

Gradually, knowledge has replaced love, machines have killed imagination. No wonder that in his rare moments of lucidity, man is seized by fear and anguish: *Who* am I? And *where* am I?

For the Jew, the problem is particularly pertinent and poignant. No elaborations are necessary. Since our beginnings, with rare exceptions, we have been considered strangers. We have come to exemplify—by our very existence—other peoples' prejudices toward their strangers. We know their attitude toward us—what is *our* attitude toward them? And how are the two linked? Are we to remain strangers forever?

WHO IS A STRANGER? What is a stranger? Scripture offers three terms which could serve as definitions: *ger,* *nochri,* and *zar.* The same three notions have undergone dramatic change in Talmudic literature.

In the Bible, *ger* and *nochri* indicate legal and geographical factors, while *zar* is related mainly to spiritual and religious ones.

A *ger* is the stranger who lives among Jews, meaning, on Jewish land, in Jewish surroundings, in a Jewish atmosphere; but he has not adopted the Jewish faith although he has acquired Jewish customs, values, and friends.

A *nochri* is a *ger* who, for reasons of his own, wishes to remain aloof or separated. The *ger* adjusts and even assimilates, while the *nochri* wants to remain different, an outsider—though a friendly one.

As for the *zar*, he is even further removed. He is not only different but hostile.

Hence, in our ancient tradition, we were extremely hospitable toward the *ger* and even the *nochri*— and extremely severe with the *zar*, who, by the way, was not really a stranger, for while the terms *ger* and *nochri* refer to Gentiles, *zar* applies to Jews.

The *ger* seems to have been a special person, endowed with all kinds of gifts. He was frequently found in the good company of the Levi—the Levite—who ranks just below the priest. Both enjoy exceptional privileges. One must be as charitable to the *ger* as to the Levite. One must not reject the *ger* or cause him harm or loss or distress; one must extend more assistance to him—or her—than to the average person; one must make an effort to understand the *ger* and make him feel welcome, at home; one must love him—or her. The term *veahavta*—and you shall love—is used three times in Scripture: And you shall love your God with all your heart; you shall love your fellow man; and you shall love the *ger*, the stranger.

In Scripture, it develops into almost an obsession. It is stressed again and again—persistently, endlessly— that we must love the *ger*. And we are told why: we have all been strangers in Egypt. That is precisely what

Abraham heard in his vision of the covenant. In other words: we must not treat others the way we have been treated. We must show them compassion, charity, and love. Above all, we must not make them *feel* like strangers. All the Jewish laws, with very few exceptions, apply to the ger. Those of *Shabbat*, of holidays, of Yom Kippur—yes, he must fast on the Day of Atonement. He must not feel left out. He is protected, perhaps overprotected, by the law. He must be given special treatment, special attention, special consideration; he is someone special. So much so that in time the term *ger* came to mean convert or proselyte, a *ger-tzedek*: a just convert, or perhaps a convert *to* justice; someone who joins our people not lightheartedly, for superficial reasons, but out of conviction, out of belief that despite the suffering and persecutions, or because of them, Judaism is inspired by truth and embodies the supreme quest for justice.

Thus, in Talmudic literature, which discourages conversion, the *ger* is generally praised and even exalted, honored, and rewarded. He is made into a superior person to whom nothing is denied. We offer him not only a past—our own—but eternity as well. We assure him that on Passover eve, at the Seder, he may declare—for all to hear—that his fathers and forefathers were slaves in Egypt; and that, like all of us, he was freed by Moses; like all of us, he stood at Sinai and received God's word and His law. We go so far as to declare that our God favors him over us. And Rabbi

Shimon ben Lakish explains why. We Jews accepted the Law under duress; we had no choice—while the convert comes to God on his own.

The *ger*'s position was so privileged in the Talmud that Moses objected: Why compare him to the Levite? Why does he deserve such honor? And again, God used the argument of the *ger*'s purity of heart: What didn't I have to do to persuade the people of Israel to accept my Law? I had to free them from bondage, feed them in the desert, protect them from their enemies, impress them with continuous miracles, one greater than the other, one more astonishing than the other—while the *ger*, the convert, didn't need all these signals—I didn't even call him, and yet he came.

And so he occupies a higher position than the born Jew. There are things we may not do to him—or even say to him. We may not remind him of his past—so as not to embarrass him. Anyway, his past is now the same as ours. The *ger* can achieve whatever God chooses not to do: he—and he alone—can change his past.

Furthermore, every *ger* may claim direct kinship with Abraham—the first convert, the father of all converts—whose greatest virtue was to expose other people to his faith. The *ger* is even linked to the Messiah, who, as the son of David, will be a descendant of a convert—Ruth.

Abraham's mission was to attract *gerim*—that's why he traveled so far and wandered so often. The

Midrash compares him and his wanderings to a bottle of perfume: it must be shaken to spread its fragrance. Later, the Talmud says, Jewish exile had a similar motivation: while wandering through the world, driven from city to city, from village to village, the people of Israel disseminated God's words, God's truth.

But Abraham was not only a *ger* in the religious sense; he was also a stranger in the geographical sense—the first *Jewish* stranger—one who, because of his *Jewishness*, had to endure the hardships of alienation and expatriation. No wonder, then, that in his vision of the covenant he anxiously saw his people become a people of refugees to whom others would *not* be charitable.

Quite the contrary.

For there exists a fundamental difference between the Jewish attitude toward strangers, and that of other peoples.

THE STRANGER, on the sociological and human level, is someone who suggests the unknown, the prohibited, the beyond; he seduces, he attracts, he wounds—and leaves; he is someone who comes from places you have never visited—and never will—sent by dark powers who know more about you than you know about them, and who resent you for being what you are, where you are, or simply—for being. The stranger represents what you are not, what you cannot be, simply because you are not *he*. Between you and him no contact seems possible, except through suspicion, terror, or repulsion. The stranger is *the other*. He is not bound by your laws, by your memories; his language is not yours, nor his silence. He is an emissary of evil and violence. Or of death. Surely he is from the other side.

Thus in many traditions he was, in fact, rejected, isolated, condemned. He was the nomad looking for water and wine; the Gypsy asking for a place to sing; the beggar searching for a roof; the fugitive seeking shelter; the madman haunted by shadows. Whether seeking consolation or forgetfulness, the stranger was sent away or somehow disposed of. The tribe wished to stay closed—unified. Pure. The stranger, bearer of an evil omen, could only undermine the established order. He had to be expelled. Or exorcised. Or even killed.

Or, in more enlightened civilizations, he had to be absorbed, meaning—assimilated. Disarmed, undressed, transformed. He would be welcome to stay, but only after giving up his name, his past, his memories, his bonds with his own people; a Jew, for example, had to become Christian, or Moslem, or Communist—or whatever. He would be offered the possibility of living, and living happily, provided he paid the inevitable *rite de passage*, which was a kind of metamorphosis or transsubstantiation. You wish to be with us? Be one of us.

There was yet another, more radical, method, one practiced and perfected by the Nazis. With them, the fear of the stranger, the hate for the stranger reached climactic proportions. His very presence evoked ancient suspicions and ancestral frustrations. In the Third Reich, cultural or religious transformation ceased to be an option. The stranger had to be disfigured. Shamed. Diminished. Erased. More cruel than pagans or cannibals had ever been, the Nazi executioners wanted to dehumanize their victims before killing them: the stranger had to become an object.

Only Islam—because of its link with Abraham— sometimes showed more compassion and hospitality toward strangers. Islam is, after all, a religion of people who for centuries wandered from tribe to tribe, from oasis to oasis, in search of water and shade. But even though Islam is an exception, its hospitality toward its guests extended only over short periods of time: how long can you be a guest? Ultimately the guests became strangers once more and had to choose exile, death, or conversion—for Islam means submission. The stranger had to submit—or die. The stranger as a sovereign individual seems to have been incompatible with the inner sovereignty of all traditions—except the Jewish one.

To us, too, the stranger represents the unknown; but the attraction he holds over us is one of curiosity and fascination—not hate. Rather than absorb the stranger, we encourage him to remain independent and true to his genuine self; we want him to maintain his identity and enrich it. Except for one or two periods in our history, we discouraged conversion. Under Yannai there were forced conversions—and we lived to regret it under Herod, whose reign was the bloodiest in Judea.

Judaism teaches us that man must be authentic, and that he can find his authenticity only within his own culture and tradition. We don't want to make Jews out of Christians; we want to make Jews out of Jews, and to help Christians to be better Christians. We want the stranger to offer us not what we already have—or whatever we may have given him—but that which *he* has and *we* don't. We don't want him to resemble us any more than we wish to resemble him. We look at him hoping to find his uniqueness, to understand that which makes him different—that which makes him a stranger.

For man, aware of both his limitations and his desire to transcend them, recognizes that the stranger forces him to call into question not only his own judgments of himself but also his relations with others. Faced with the unknown, we realize that every consciousness represents the unknown to everyone else. God, and God alone, remains Himself in all His relationships—never becoming someone else, never becoming *the other*.

And yet, just as man can attain his ultimate truth only through other human beings, God can be united to His creation only through man. Man needs the other to be human—just as God needs man to be God.

For the Jew, the stranger suggests a world to be lived in, to be enhanced, or saved. One awaits the stranger, one welcomes him, one is grateful to him for his presence. What was Abraham's greatness? He invited into his home all strangers, be they angels or fugitives, and made them feel welcome. Rabbi Eliezer, the father of the Besht, became a father because of his hospitality toward unknown wanderers. In the Jewish tradition, the stranger may very well be someone important: a prophet in disguise, one of the hidden just men. Or even the Messiah. He is to be accepted for what he is, the way he is. Thus we hope to receive a fragment of his secret knowledge, a spark of his flame—a key to his secret.

The question therefore is, How should the contact, the exchange, occur? What should its nature be? Am I to approach the stranger in his language or mine? On his level or mine? In other words: Must I make an effort to resemble him so as to better discover him? The answer, naturally, is, no. For that would mean accepting his terms; that would mean submission and defeat, leading—finally—to dissolution rather than to affirmation of our identity.

Now, we realize that there is in man precisely such a desire, calling for this kind of end, this kind of death. A desire to break with his surroundings, burn his bridges, deny his past and his experiences, plunge into the mass of humanity and go under . . . thus solving the problem of existence by putting an end to that existence. It is a desire to become another, to live the life of another, the destiny of another, assume the death of another—to die as a stranger in order to forget pain, shame, guilt, in order to disappear—to commit either physical or spiritual suicide.

That urge may or may not be rooted in weakness. Man may feel helpless to adjust to the image he has of himself and so wish to adopt the image the stranger has of him; ultimately he may try to resemble the stranger—or even the enemy.

But then it may also be related to a more positive passion—his need to renew himself, to replenish himself. He may leave his land, his home, his habits, in the hope that as an expatriate he may have greater opportunities to rethink, reevaluate, and redefine his place and role under the sun.

And so the stranger gets up one morning and without saying goodbye to anyone, disappears. He goes underground, joins a counterculture; he seeks out places and societies whose languages he does not understand, whose laws are alien—but those things don't frighten him. On the contrary: he wants *not* to understand, *not* to know. For what he knows, he does not like; and what he understands, he does not accept. He has chosen exile so as to be someone else—a stranger—and thus to discover a new expression of truth, a new way of living out the human condition in its ever-changing forms.

That is why he is always on the run. Everywhere he leaves one more mask, one more memory. In order to become a total stranger, he must reject the last vestiges of his former self. Sometimes it ends well: Abraham did break with his parents to become Abraham, Moses did leave the royal palace to become the leader of leaders. Later, much later, mystics chose exile to achieve anonymity; Hasidic masters became vagabonds; poets sought poverty and adventure. Sometimes it ends badly: Philo of Alexandria, Josephus Flavius, Spinoza, Otto Weininger, and even Heine and Bergson—all were attracted by the other side and, to different degrees, went too far and became estranged from their people. They were not prudent enough. So taken were they by the stranger that they became strangers themselves . . . to themselves.

What went wrong? They could not resist the stranger's temptations. They forgot that we are supposed—and indeed commanded—to love the stranger as long as he fulfills his role, meaning, as long as his mystery challenges our certainties and forces us to reexamine our own values, our own sincerity—as long as the stranger represents the question; but if and when he attempts to force his answers upon us, he must be opposed. He can be of help only as a stranger—lest you are ready to become his caricature. And your own. The virtue of the *ger* is that he remains a *ger*. Though he may have become Jewish in all aspects, he retains his superior quality of *ger-tzedek*, a just convert, for ten generations: we would not deprive him of that which made the stranger in him become our brother.

Now—WHAT ABOUT the second category: the *nochri?* He clearly ranks below the *ger*. He remains actively on the outside—and there is something negative about his remaining there. We are told to love the *ger*—but no mention is made about love for the *nochri*. On the contrary: we underline their differences so as to distinguish between them. We are allowed to lend money with interest to the *nochri*, but not to the *ger*. Ritually impure meat may be given to the *ger*, but must be sold to the *nochri*.

Why this distinction? Both terms mean "stranger." But while *ger* indicates a movement, an impulse *toward* the Jew, *nochri* indicates the opposite: a movement *away* from the Jew.

Nochri stems from the word *nechar*—abroad, elsewhere. Variants of that word mean to deny, to remove oneself from the community, to alienate oneself from the family or group—while a variant of *ger* means the opposite: to come closer, to join, to convert.

There is something in the term *nochri* which implies a will, a deliberate plan, to be estranged: a *nochri* is one who could ultimately use his status as stranger to oppose you, to rule you.

While a *ger*, at least in Scripture, is merely an alien resident—one who came from far away to share your joys and sorrows—the *nochri* has come on a temporary basis. Tomorrow he may leave with something of us, his prey; he has always been, and will continue to be, attached to another home, another system. Even when he is with you, he is elsewhere.

Hence Abraham's pronouncement that among strangers he was a *ger* but never a *nochri*. Even with people very different from himself, he was really there, with them—as was Joseph in Egypt, who claims that even among *nochrim*, the Jew remains a *ger*. A Jew may not be a *nochri* to anyone, meaning, he may not use his Jewishness to attack, to humiliate, to negate anyone else.

But a Jew can belong to the third category—the worst of all: a Jew, only a Jew, can be a *zar*.

Zar, too, means stranger—and his lot in Scripture is worse than that of the other two. We are told to love the *ger* and be kind and generous to him. The *nochri*, God shields. God offers him protection. Not so the *zar*.

Who is a *zar*? Originally the term applied to those Jews who were kept outside the Temple. Then the Prophets used it to describe the profane, the alien, the destructive elements in our midst.

Zar is the Jew who remains a stranger to other Jews—and to the Jew in himself. The term implies a religious and metaphysical opposition to his own identity; a Jew who loathes his Jewishness is a *zar*—the worst of enemies. That is why most injunctions against the *zar* are extremely severe. He may not eat from priestly sacrificial offerings; they are so sacred that he may not even come close—too dangerous. A *zar*—the destructive stranger—uses his faith as a weapon, a faith that is not really his own: he has usurped it from others.

The term *zar* is therefore totally derogatory. Thoughts that are *zarot*, unholy, must be discarded. Aaron's two sons perished because they introduced *esh zarah*—an unholy fire—into the sanctuary. When God expresses his dissatisfaction, his disgust with certain human actions, he says they are *lezarah li*, they are all alien to me, meaning, they repel me, they anger me.

Why such hostility toward this kind of stranger? The answer is obvious: he represents danger.

For there are many ways to live as strangers—and they are not all alike.

To act as a stranger toward strangers is natural. It may be unpleasant, painful and absurd to find oneself face to face with someone one has never seen and *know* that the relationship is one of individuals whom fate has brought together for one moment, one encounter. A word, a gesture—and the moment is forgotten.

But then again: I could conceivably be a stranger to a friend—a colleague, a fellow writer—even a brother. Cain and Abel were not enemies; they were strangers, which is worse. To reject or be rejected by a friend is painful. Here I am, there he is; and I thought we belonged to the same intimate circle; that we were allies, bound by the same dreams and discoveries—and suddenly I am confronted with a stranger. I thought I could count on him. I thought I counted for him. Wrong. When I see the stranger *in* him, it also means that I am a stranger *to* him.

This is serious, but there is something even more serious—to realize that I am a stranger to myself, which means that there is a stranger in me who wants to live my life or my death—or even to die by pushing me to my death through self-hate. This stranger forces me to look at things, events, and myself with *his* eyes, urging me to give up because of him.

One must never allow oneself to become this kind of stranger. To anybody. During the era of night and flame, the executioner wanted not only to kill us as strangers—anonymously—but as numbers, as objects, not as human beings. He wanted to kill us twice—to kill the humanity in us before killing us.

And yes—there were times when nocturnal processions of tired, frightened people would march to the mass graves and then lie down quietly, obediently, almost respectfully. Those men and women were dead before they were killed. But even worse: the killers tried to drive the victims to self-hate, pushing them to see themselves through the killers' eyes—thus to become strangers to themselves, strangers to be despised, discarded. In this the killers did not succeed. Few Jews became *zar* in ghettos and death camps.

Do not believe what some scholars and writers

tell you: the Jews did not collaborate in their own death; they were not overcome by a collective passion for self-destruction.

Who is the enemy? He has a name: Amalek—the eternal stranger.

Remember: in our Biblical tradition, real strangers are treated with some measure of fairness. Esau? We feel compassion for him. Pharaoh? In spite of his cruel edicts, we somehow are unable to hate him, or even be angry with him: after all, it was God who hardened his heart. Poor Pharaoh: God's instrument and Israel's victim. Or take Balaam: he cannot even curse us. He starts to form words, rhymes, sentences, he thinks he can blacklist all the Jews and involuntarily ends up singing their praise: poor prophet, poor poet. The only enemy to inspire unqualified apprehension and anger is . . . Amalek. Always. We are unmistakably ordered to strike him, to defeat him, to kill him.

Why Amalek? Amalek, we said, is the stranger who frightens us most, the stranger who knows our weakness and—perhaps—*is* our weakness.

Though we know much about other ancient peoples with whom our forefathers were dealing, we know little about Amalek. All we know is that we are told to remember to wipe out the memory of him. Meaning, we must forget him, but remember what he tried to do to us. He attacked women and children—defenseless people. He attacked when we were weak. As soon as Israel doubted God's presence in its midst, as soon as Israel felt apprehensive about its destiny, Amalek launched his assault. Amalek: the epitome of the stranger. Amalek: the other side of experience, of life, of hope, of ecstasy. He is *the other*; he exists not simply to force us to be strong, to teach us the art of survival; no: he exists to kill us, to turn us into victims of our own weakness. Amalek: the stranger in us, who is against us; he must be opposed mercilessly. And struck down.

LET US RECAPITULATE: these are the differences between our traditional Jewish attitude toward the stranger and that of others who were taught to oppress, repress, or altogether eliminate the stranger they confronted. As for us, we have tried to resist the stranger *inside* ourselves. When others were complacent with themselves and ruthless to strangers, we did the opposite. We have been and are compassionate toward others—except for Amalek.

We are compassionate even toward the enemy—except the enemy whose aim is to annihilate the Jew in us. That is the Jewish belief. If I must die, I shall, but I must, to the last minute, resist death—and resist the enemy who symbolizes death. To wish to die is the ultimate insult to our existence. That is why suicide is a sin: we may not allow the enemy inside us—the stranger inside us—to choose death on our behalf.

And now, in conclusion, let us return to Abraham, who, on that dramatic and suspenseful night, learned for the first time what the future held for his children. He saw the fire and the smoke; the exile. He saw the darkness and he felt the anguish. On that night he shared the experiences of our generation. On that night he signed, on our behalf, the covenant—a symbol of endurance and survival.

Our generation can best understand the terms of the covenant. We have seen the smoking furnace, we have seen the burning torch. And night has no end. And Abraham's sacrificial offerings were not saved. Of all the divine promises, only one was fulfilled: We have not become strangers to our past. Now we are waiting—again—for the rest of the covenant to be implemented. We are waiting. . . .

We asked earlier: Why did Abraham agree to its terms? Why didn't he plead with God to save his descendants from exile? To spare them from slavery? What better time could there have been to ask and obtain compassion for his children? Why didn't he say, *Ribono shel olam*, Master of the universe, the covenant must be agreed upon by both of us—and I shall not agree unless you accept my conditions? But then, God, too, causes us to wonder: Was that the proper moment to tell His partner that his children would be cast into exile? That they would become strangers? Wasn't He worried that Abraham might become frightened and discouraged—to the point of refusing the terms of the covenant?

Yes, Abraham was frightened: the text says so. But his fear didn't last. Yes, he felt anguish when God first revealed that his descendants would become strangers. But then he heard the last part of the sentence: they will be strangers in foreign lands. Among strangers. Not at home. Not to themselves.

And so Abraham felt reassured. He understood that the covenant contained a plan, a kind of blueprint for life in society. A society without strangers would be impoverished; to live only amongst ourselves, constantly inbreeding, never facing an outsider to make us question again and again our certainties and rules, would inevitably lead to atrophy. The experience of encountering a stranger—like the experience of suffering—is important and creative, provided we know when to step back.

In His promise, God told Abraham that his children would always know how far they could go. They would be strangers only among strangers, to strangers, but not to Him. They would return to Him—as His children. And this too is part of the covenant.

Exile will come to an end—everything does; exile will have a meaning—everything has, for God is also in exile, God is everywhere. God is not a stranger to His creation and surely not to His people. *El* is in Isra*el*: God is in Jewish history, therefore in history. And man must not treat Him as a stranger—or be a stranger to Him.

Of course, we are all strangers on this earth which

is older than we are—and yet it is up to us to be true to ourselves, to live our own lives and share them, to bear our truth and our fervor and share them—and then one day we may all gather around one who has not come as yet—but who *will* come.

And on that day, when he does come—finally—he will not be a stranger—and none of us will ever be strangers again. For he will be—the Messiah.

A Celebration
of Friendship

WHAT IS A FRIEND? It is my character Gabriel who, in
The Gates of the Forest asks himself this question out
loud. And he answers: "More than a father, more than
a brother, a traveling companion; with him, you can
achieve what seemed impossible, even if you must lose
it later. Friendship marks a life even more deeply than
love. Love risks degenerating into obsession; friendship
is never anything but sharing. It is to a friend that you
communicate the awakening of desire, the birth of a
vision or a terror, the anguish of seeing the sun disappear or of finding that order and justice are no more.
Is the soul immortal, and, if so, why are we afraid to
die? If God exists, how can we lay claim to freedom,
since He is its beginning and its end? What is death?
The closing of a parenthesis, and nothing more? And

what about life? In the mouth of a philosopher, these questions may have a false ring, but asked by friends during adolescence they have the power to change. What is a friend? Someone who for the first time makes you aware of your loneliness and his, and helps you to escape so you in turn can help him. Thanks to him you may remain silent without shame and speak freely without risk."

Gabriel is my friend and he speaks for me. All my fictional characters exalt friendship; for some it is an obsession. Sometimes I tell myself that I have made them up only because I needed to believe in friendship, because I needed them as friends.

As a child, I felt so weak, so inadequate, that I'd spend my pocket money to make a new friend or keep a playmate. In this I was following the counsel of the Talmudic sage Rabbi Yehoshua, son of Prakhia, who, in *Ethics of the Fathers* invites man to *choose* for himself a Master and to acquire for himself a friend.

Nothing was ever left of the goodies and cakes I took to school—my mother lived in fear that I would faint from hunger. I distributed everything among my schoolmates. I coveted the attention of the brilliant students, the protection of the strong ones, and the affection of them all. Most of all I dreaded finding myself excluded, an outsider, alone.

I felt guilty because my friends were poor. So was I, but I was not aware of it. I wanted to obtain forgiveness for what I believed to be my privileged circumstances. To make amends, I gave away whatever I was given. All by myself, I hoped to do away with social barriers and the injustice that springs from them; I burned to correct the errors of creation. I deprived myself of the superfluous to provide for the needy. I arrived with full pockets and went home with empty hands.

I remember the friends of my childhood as I remember my childhood; I look at them as I look at myself, and a familiar sadness engulfs me. Where are they? Why were we separated? How could I have deserved to outlive them? For most of them are no longer of this world.

I recall them and I speak to them: Do you remember? Our schemes, our dreams of long ago seem closer to me than the events of today. Our teachers, so strict they terrorized us; the tears we tried to choke back as we struggled with some indecipherable text; our anguished or ecstatic faces at the sight of a beggar who told strange and marvelous tales: how could I forget them? Our walks through the forest on a Saturday afternoon, our preparations for Passover, our Purim games: it was yesterday.

What did our friendship mean to us? We were still so small, we hardly knew the real significance of the word. We were pals, that was all. Together we learned to read, to write, to pray; we amused ourselves by gathering fruit in spring, by counting clouds, by outwitting our tutors or supervisors at the synagogue.

Of course, one malicious word, one rough gesture, would make me sob with vexation, but the next day everything was forgotten.

For children, friendship takes on a practical, immediate meaning: You give me your toy, you are my friend; if you don't, you aren't. It's all very simple. And provisional. A friend turns into an enemy and back into a friend in an instant. Is this to say that their feelings are less profound? I would rather say that, for children, time passes less quickly: one instant in a child's life is like a year in ours.

Friendship takes on more breadth, another dimension, when a child enters adolescence: then, it becomes a necessity. Without it, he suffocates.

The adolescent begins to question himself, that is, he opens himself to anguish. He asks himself questions, he demands answers. Alert to the world that eludes him, he wants to be able to think that his case, at least, is not unique: all men are weak, vulnerable; they end up bowing their heads in resignation; they end up being drawn into death as one is drawn into a hypnotic gaze. The adolescent is not an individualist. Even when he wishes to be different, he hopes to be like others; that is, he wants to be different because this is what everybody wants. He is comforted by the words "Me too"; I hurt: "Me too"; I am in love but she does not love me: "Me too"; I love God, but He does not answer me: "Me too." The friend, for the adolescent, is the one who says, "Me too."

I vividly remember the friends of my adolescence. I see us sitting on a bench, rocking back and forth the better to concentrate during our study and prayer. I hear us chanting a Talmudic text or a mystical litany. I see the son of a Hasidic rabbi who speaks to me in our garden of a secret army to drive away our enemies; I walk in the courtyard of a synagogue with the son of a merchant who refuses to speak any language but Hebrew. Absorbed in ourselves, we do not hear the sounds of war in the distance, the sounds of the enemy who advances on us. Our parents take an interest in politics, in what goes on at the front—not we. We are interested in what goes on in heaven. The present leaves us cold; only eternity excites us.

Well, yes, at the time I was too young to understand that eternity does not exist except in relation to the present. I was not mature enough to understand that it is eternity which lends this moment its mystery and its distinction. There were many things I did not understand. That is why I needed the presence of a friend at my side: to share my confusion.

Let us take a look at Scripture: What role does it attribute to friendship? And, first of all, where is friendship to be found in it? It is hardly ever mentioned, at least not explicitly. There are references to solidarity, love, hate, vengeance, punishment, and promises—but very few to friendship. And yet it does exist, it dominates the relationships between certain Biblical characters. Unfortunately, these are not al-

ways on the side of the angels. In fact, close friend-
ships are usually found among the "bad guys." The
people who tried to erect the Tower of Babel showed
more solidarity than those who followed Moses out
of Egypt. Datan and Aviram, who organized the plot
against God and His messenger, were close friends,
while the entourage of Moses was divided by internal
squabbles. Only Joshua and Caleb, son of Jefune, who
were friends at the time of their reconnaissance mission into Canaan, remained friends. There are no
other examples in Scripture. The same is true of the
"brothers" mentioned in the Bible. Cain and Abel,
Jacob and Esau, Joseph and his brothers all illustrate
a cruel and timeless truth: human beings can become
enemies and each other's victims even if they are
brothers. Any exceptions? Yes: Moses and Aaron.
Moses learns that his brother has been elevated to
the office of High Priest and he is delighted with the
news. And yet, one remembers, his brother had caused
him no small worry, no little grief. Never mind: Moses
has not forgotten but he forgives. Aaron is not only
his brother; he is also his partner, his friend.

Still, it is not the story of Moses and Aaron that
is usually cited to illustrate friendship between two
men in Biblical history. Whenever selfless and complete friendship is celebrated, the names evoked are
those of David and Jonathan. Jonathan knows that
Saul, his father, both loves and hates David, yet he
remains David's friend and protects him against Saul.

Jonathan's loyalty to the future king is absolute. The two men understand each other down to the slightest gesture. They are always on the same side, they fight for the same cause. One could say the same soul lives in both of them. As adolescents, we sought to imitate David and Jonathan, who stood together against the world of adults with its plots and intrigues—sometimes spiritual, at other times banal. Friendship was to protect us and make us strong.

MY FRIENDS AND I needed strength for what we hoped to accomplish. What was it we had in mind? As I described in one of my novels, the three of us intended to accelerate the course of events and hasten the coming of the Messiah. Laugh if you will, but for us it was serious. Having studied the splendors and the dazzling mysteries of the Kabbala under the guidance of a Master whose physical weakness belied his spiritual power, we were convinced we would find the right words, the appropriate gestures, to liberate the Jewish people and, through them, all the nations from the exile in which humanity is held prisoner. For us, impassioned and exalted adolescents that we were in our little village in the Carpathian mountains, this was a most serious matter.

I remember my two friends, I shall remember them always. I see their burning faces, the penetrating look in their eyes. I see us at the House of Study at night, huddled in shadows, making of our project and our friendship an offering to Zion, in need of solace. I hear my friends whispering the litanies of Yehuda Halevi. I feel their pain as they can feel mine. I see us going home in the small hours, in silence.

We had vowed to one another to go to the end of our mystical quest, even if it meant risking madness, isolation, or death. We had promised to keep our intentions secret. Mad, yes: we were mad as only certain adolescents, certain friends, can be. One had to be mad to believe it was in man's power to conquer evil, to disarm death; one had to be mad to believe that one need only utter certain phrases, mortify the body in a certain way, invoke certain celestial powers, to bring redemption. In the end, it was not the Messiah who arrived, it was his nemesis: the killer, the mass murderer, the exterminator of nations. As for my two friends, I saw them go; there was a contemplative air about them, as if they were meditating upon the meaning of their lives and mine, upon the failure of our adventure in bringing the Messiah. I saw them from the back, leaving the ghetto as if drawn by night.

I followed them a week later. That is to say, I followed them as far as the kingdom of barbed wire, but I did not see them again: they had been liquidated a few hours after their arrival, along with the other sick people in their convoy.

Ever since, I have been looking for them. I have never stopped looking for them. Other friends have come to enrich my life, but not one has resembled either of them. When they left they took with them not only a conception of Messianic hope, but also the ideal of friendship.

My new friends and I try to understand what has happened to our people, and sometimes even to act upon its destiny, but my mystical experiences of long ago remain enveloped in memory.

In other words: friendship has not disappeared from my life; it has only changed in nature. Even in a universe of ultimate horror friendship was a haven.

Of course, the technicians of death tried to deprive us of it. Everyone for himself, they told us. Forget your parents, your brothers, your past, or else you will perish. That is what they kept telling us day and night. But what happened was the opposite. Those who lived only for themselves, only to feed themselves, ended up succumbing to the laws of death, while the others, those who knew whom to live for—a parent, a brother, a friend—managed to obey the laws of life.

I feel uncomfortable speaking of it here—I have always preferred to keep the most private matters to myself—but how could I recall my friends of those days without mentioning the best, the most devoted, the most generous of them all—my father? I lived only for him. And by him. He needed me—and I him—to live one more day, one more hour. I knew it and he knew it. I see him again and, at the core of my being, I feel a nameless sorrow: nothing has replaced that friendship.

• •

BUT IS THIS not true of any friendship? To the extent that it exists, it will continue to exist. It is its own successor, and nothing can destroy it. Is this too idealized, too optimistic a concept? I have drawn it from the movement of Hasidism, which is a celebration of friendship. No other movement puts so much emphasis on friendship. In Hasidism, friendship is as important as faith in the Masters. The disciple is enjoined not only to follow the rabbi, but also to make friends. Often the Hasid comes to the rabbi not only to see him, but to meet other disciples. Gather together—that is the Hasidic rallying cry in all its joy. Do not isolate yourself from your fellow man, but seek his affection, his love.

This was valid for the generation of the Besht, for that of the Maggid of Mezeritch, and also for ours. An uprooted Hasid will always be able to count on his friends to provide a roof for him. A despondent Hasid will soon find new resources, fervent allies who will help him to fight despair. A Hasid is never alone nor allowed to be depressed. This is permitted the rabbi, but not the disciple. What, then, is a Hasid to do who is crushed by his memories, shattered by his inability to affirm life while he mourns his dead? How can a Hasid who has lived through the long night of the concentration camps still open himself to joy, to ecstasy? Alone, he would not have the strength. With friends, he can undertake anything, relearn everything: the duty of keeping the faith, of loving, of singing, of sharing with others the salt of his life, and his secret, too, through stories and melodies, through words and silences. The unhappy Hasid will have to choose happiness so as not to be a bad influence on his friends, so as to prevent them from following him into the abyss.

Here again, need I reveal to you what some of you perhaps already know? I tried to explore this attitude in one of my first novels, *The Town Beyond the Wall*. There I told the story of a young man who accepts imprisonment and torture to save a friend who is still free. But his cellmate is a madman. And my character realizes that the torturers have placed them together deliberately. Their purpose? My character is to be infected by the sick man's madness. If he does not act, he too will lose his reason. So, in order not to sink into insanity, he goes about healing the madman—his brother, his friend.

A great Hasidic Master, Rabbi Moshe-Leib of Sassov, said of sacred love: If you want to find the spark, you must look among the ashes.

Peretz Markish

AFTER A LECTURE on Talmud in Geneva, a young man timidly approached me and said he wanted to speak to me. He was Simon Markish, eldest son of the great Jewish poet Peretz Markish.

I had just published my novel *The Testament*, in which I tried to evoke the lives and deaths of the Communist Jewish writers, novelists, and poets murdered on Stalin's orders in 1952.

My principal character, Paltiel Kossover, brought together diverse elements in each of these Communist Jewish writers: their passion for justice, their thirst for fraternity, their love for the poor, for the disinherited. They intrigued me.

I could not understand: How can a real Jew—that is, someone who seeks self-definition by and through his Jewish condition—succumb to the Communist faith, which, at the extreme, preaches total assimilation? How could a traditional Jewish intellectual like Der Nister, the great novelist of the Bratslaver Hasidim, adhere to a totalitarian party in which each member sings praises to a leader as if he were God? How could a poet as gifted as Peretz Markish defer to the fanaticism of Stalin? How could these men of heart and intelligence, educated in the Jewish messianic tradition, take on the roles of soldiers of Communism? And then there was something else I could not understand: What made Stalin slaughter them? Why this fierce hatred? I studied published and unpublished documents. I questioned Communists of that period. I wanted to know, and I wrote the novel as much to learn as to inform.

Of all the writers, two fascinated me in particular: Markish and Der Nister. First, because I admired their talent—the romantic inspiration of one, the poetic power of the other. I hoped to discover who they were beyond their words.

"Perhaps you knew my father?" asked Simon Markish at my lecture in Geneva. I looked at him for a long moment. Was the son a poet as well?

"No," I said, "I never knew your father."

He seemed surprised. "But in your book, you speak of him so well. It is as though . . ."

I interrupted him. "No, I never met Peretz Markish, but I love him very much."

In fact, Paltiel Kossover was inspired as much by Markish as by Der Nister. Not, to be sure, on the concrete level of appearances, but on a more profound level of being. Kossover drew from their source. Like them, he wanted to sing of man, and like them, he became man's victim.

Of all the responses to *The Testament*, that of Simon Markish affected me most. Need I explain the attraction his father had for me? Peretz Markish and his work are part of a landscape at once familiar and strange—that of my adolescence, in my small town of Sighet, which I believed to be the center of the universe. In his poems I found older friends who, before me, had dared to venture into the forbidden realm of action and thought that sometimes opposed religious tradition.

I began to read him, to study him, and have never had enough. His vision of man embroiled in war, yearning for simple happiness. His judgment of the enemies of the Jewish people and of all humanity affected me deeply. His warnings, his promises, his words of consolation—you cannot read them without being distressed. His voice summons and penetrates you; you will not forget him.

To know him better, I read and reread what his widow, Esther Markish, wrote of him, and what others published—commentaries on his work, or on Russian Jewish poetry in general, like those of Abraham Sutzkever and Irving Howe; memoirs, encounters, correspondence about his turbulent years before and after the Second World War.

Thus I discovered a vast literature reflecting every trend in Russian Jewish poetry: the classic conception, lyric vocation, expressionist . . . the naturalism of Bergelson, the realism of Feffer, the mysticism of Der Nister. In every corner of the Soviet Union, Jewish writers and poets, like others, sang the new hope in which the promise still seemed beautiful and pure. Naive? Possibly. In those times young Jews felt the need to believe in something new. For centuries they had suffered too much, personally and in their collective memory, not to aspire to smash all the old structures and replace them with a revolutionary system in which all would become possible.

Peretz Markish is a good example.

Born in Wolin at the end of the nineteenth century, he knew poverty, misery, and fear. He attended a Jewish school, studied the holy books, sang in synagogue, awaited the coming of the Messiah, and prayed to God to protect his people in exile. Then came the revolution, and, like so many of his contemporaries, young Markish joined its ranks. Long live liberty. Long live the future. In Communist terms this meant, Down with the past, down with religion. One must be freed from all that recalls tradition: the holidays, the customs, the laws, the songs and dreams of the past. The rabbis, the sages, the ancient philosophers must yield their place to the heralds of modern socialism. Like everyone, Markish is taken in. His writings of this period praise the Communists and condemn all who are not. He is hard on Jewish landlords, employers, and notables—excessively hard. And yet, several years later he is nevertheless taken to task by the political watchdogs of the party who criticize him for portraying only Jews . . . and then, *unlike* everyone else, he refuses to bend. He defends himself and perseveres. It is as a Jew—as a Jewish poet and as a Jewish writer— that he expresses his universal aspirations.

Is this why he leaves the Soviet Union in the 1920s? He goes to Berlin, to Warsaw, and visits Palestine. With Uri Zvi Grinberg and Meilekh Ravitch he founds *Khalastra,* a review bursting with vigor, freshness, and impertinence. He reveals himself everywhere as a brilliant and spellbinding lecturer. He challenges established ideas, unsettles all that appears secure. He questions everything. Ilya Ehrenburg describes him as a Jewish Byron, anxious, romantic, and possessed of a beauty that made one dream. He could stay in the West and build a career. What he wants, he gets. The people acclaim him; he is quoted everywhere. His humor is appealing. His courage in breaking with the traditional lyricism of Jewish poetry is praised. He triumphs. And nevertheless . . . he returns to the Soviet Union.

Why? A premonition of the rise of Nazism? He senses that Western Europe is collapsing, he foresees the destruction of the Jewish communities of Poland. He is too much of a poet not to be a little bit of a prophet as well. In Russia a sort of Jewish cultural renaissance is taking place. He publishes reviews and books in Yiddish. He teaches classes and gives lessons. Around him one finds Kvitko and Hofstein, Halkin and Feffer, and, of course, on stage, dominating them all, the great Shlomo Mikhoels. Ah, yes, one easily understands how a Jewish poet succumbs to this attention. One understands his wish to be among them.

AND WHY NOT say it? On the surface, Markish seems to be right. The Order of Lenin is bestowed on him. Writing in Yiddish must therefore be something important. The Stalin-Hitler pact? A passing episode. For the Jews, the war against Nazi Germany is the occasion for a full mobilization of forces to participate in the national and international struggle. One must read what Markish writes on the Warsaw Ghetto, on Jewish history in general, and above all, on the war against the Jews. One must read what he wrote about his own times to understand the grandeur of his soul and the profound nature of his pain.

After the war, Markish is never the same. The Communist in him lives in the shadow of the Jew that he is, and whose destiny he wants to fully assume to the end. He appears to be more closed, more solitary. His poetic meditations rejoin the prophetic, classic lyricism of his distant precursors. He writes a long poem, "The Man of Forty." He spends more time with his son Simon. He takes account of what is happening around him: his friends and companions are being arrested. Soon it will be his turn.

On the morning of January 27, 1949, they come knocking on his door.

We know nothing of what happened afterward. How did he live in prison? What did he say to his judges and torturers? What songs did he compose in *his* night? I would give much to find out. Could I have created Paltiel Kossover to share his solitude?

NOTE: *In 1989 I asked President Mikhail Gorbachev to posthumously rehabilitate Peretz Markish and the other Jewish writers executed under Stalin. In the spirit of* glasnost, *that request was granted.*

Dialogues

---

1. A CHILD AND HIS GRANDFATHER.

Long ago, I taught you fervor.
    I remember.
And passion.
    I remember.
And song.
    I remember, Grandfather.
Then sing!
    I cannot. Please understand; don't be angry with me. My gaze is burning, but all the eyes it encounters are extinguished. I dwell in a cemetery, Grandfather. Like you, I am dead; only your voice reaches me. Tell me, if I were not dead, would I hear you?

You don't hear me well; you misinterpret my teachings. You're alive, therefore live!

I am incapable of it, Grandfather. I did try in the beginning; I failed. I loved you too much; now you're gone. All those I loved, I love them still, and they are gone. I try hard to emulate them. Also to follow them.

Stop! I shall not permit this. I order you to live! In ecstasy if possible, but surely in faith! And you must sing, do you hear me? You must sing! Do you want me to help you? The last time we were together, it was for the High Holy Days of the New Year.

I remember, Grandfather.

We had gone to the Rebbe to participate in the solemn services. The disciples were weeping, the Rebbe was not. He remained silent. We recited our prayers and our litanies; we implored the heavens to protect us, to let us live, we shed unending tears; not he, not the Rebbe. He may have had some inkling of what was to come and that it was too late: the decree had been signed, it was irrevocable.

But then, why was he silent? If he knew, he should have wept all the more!

At one point, just before the sounding of the shofar, he began to sing, something he had never done before.

Now I recall: his song tore at our insides.

The words, do you remember them?

No. Only the melody.

A verse from the Psalms. "The dead do not sing the Lord's praise. . . ." Oh, yes, the Rebbe knew. And therefore he tried to do the impossible: to revoke the edict. If you kill your people, if you condone its annihilation, who will praise you? Who will sanctify you with song? He sang with all his heart, with all his soul, sensing that it was for the last time. That's what we had failed to understand. For us this was the first time. Of all the men, of all the women present, you are the only survivor, the only one to carry His song in you: let it burst forth, let it ascend to heaven. Sing in His place and in mine!

I cannot, Grandfather. Don't push me to do the impossible. My place is with you, my heart is in mourning. They have murdered the child that I was, and you want me to sing?

I want you to live.

Try to understand me, Grandfather. Try to forgive me.

2. A CHILD AND HIS GRANDMOTHER.

Beneath your clothes, you were wearing your shroud.

Of course.

You had a premonition? You knew that the train was carrying us to our death?

Of course.

You should have told us.

Who would have listened? An old woman's delusions, that's what they would have called it.

You were beautiful that day, Grandmother. Calm, peaceful.

All of them were afraid. I wasn't. Fear is like pain. It hurts, it hurts very much, and suddenly it no longer hurts; you are beyond pain. And fear.

You were smiling. Like . . .

Shabbat eve?

No. Like Friday mornings. On my way home from *cheder*, breathless, I would stop by to see you. You held out the *challah*. Quickly, I washed my hands; quickly, I recited the customary prayer; quickly I bit into the warm bread. And you, Grandmother, you would sit there, in the kitchen, your black scarf on your head, watching me, smiling, and to me your smile was a haven: it announced *Shabbat* and its joy, *Shabbat* and the angels of peace that escort it into time and even into the heart of man.

That last Friday, do you remember it?

I shall remember it to the end of my days, Grandmother. We were already in the ghetto.

We were a little cramped but we were not sad.

We didn't know.

I did. Yes, I did. On that particular Friday I put the dough into the oven the same as always, and when I took it out it was charred. I tried again. Failure after failure. I was unable to produce even the tiniest chal-lah. *Then I knew.*

And yet you seemed serene.

You forget. You didn't see me. You entered the kitchen and I turned my back to you. So as not to see you, so as not to be seen by you. I handed you a piece of cake. You asked, But where is the challah? *I an-swered, We must keep it for tonight, for the* Shabbat *meal.*

But that evening, I remember, you seemed at peace.

It was already Shabbat. *I thought, It's our last here, the last with my grandson and his parents. The last* Shabbat *of my life. What good will it do to pro-test? I chose resignation, submission to His will. In a sense I even experienced a strange satisfaction. I no longer loved the world and those who live in it; I no longer loved Creation.*

That Sunday you wrapped yourself in your shroud underneath your clothes.

I felt like attending my own funeral. Only there was no funeral. God turned away from earth; in its stead He chose fire. What? You don't know? God saw somebody set the world on fire, and He began to cry so that His tears might douse the flames. But His eyes were dry.

3. A CHILD AND A STRANGER.

Stranger, tell me a story.

Look away, my boy. To look at me is dangerous.
I bring bad luck.

Tell me a story. Any story. I cannot live without
stories.

Don't listen, my boy. Close your ears. To listen
to me is dangerous. My words wound. They will dis-
tress you, they will tear you apart. Go, find someone
else to talk to, someone else to be with.

It is you who interest me, only you.

Why? Do I remind you of someone?

Perhaps.

Your father?

Possibly. I have forgotten what he looked like.

Your brother?

I've forgotten him too. I've forgotten everything,
stranger. I wish to listen to you in order to rebuild my
memory as others rebuild their careers or their lives.

You wish me to hand you my past, is that it?

Yes, that's it.

Even if it is filled with horror?

Nothing frightens me, stranger.

And what if I told you that I am Death?

I'd refuse to believe you.

Why?

Death never gives, it only takes.

You are so young, yet you spoke of Death like an old man.

I am old, older than you, older than my old Masters of long ago. At his death, my father had not reached my age.

And what if I told you that I am your father?

I would answer that you're lying.

And what if I gave you proof?

You're a stranger; my father was my father.

But your father is dead. You just told me so. Why couldn't he come back as a stranger?

The dead don't come back; we go toward them. They are waiting for us. My father is waiting for me.

You are trying to join him, is that right?

I am looking for myself near him. We lived together too short a time. I miss him.

He was strong?

Sometimes.

Wise?

Often.

Generous?

Always.

You see, my boy: it's you who are telling me stories.

I know. I couldn't live without stories.

Told to a stranger?

Told by a stranger.
>*And what if I told you* . . .

Don't say another word.

4. A CHILD AND HIS MOTHER.

I saw you, you know.

. . .

I saw you in the crowd.

. . .

The crowd was withdrawing, just as the dark sea recedes from the shore.

. . .

I didn't know.
>*What didn't you know?*

That it was the last time I would see you.
>*Yes, the last time.*

You didn't turn around.

. . .

Not even once.

. . .

Why didn't you try? Tell me! Why didn't you try to look back at me? I wanted so much to see you, to see you one last time.
>*We were being pushed. Slowly, relentlessly, the tide was carrying us forward.*

I know, I know. But still. I lack that image: you seeking me, you looking at me.

. . .

On the train, an hour earlier—or was it a week? A lifetime? You were telling us we must stay together, no matter what, we must stay together. Someone, Grandmother perhaps, was whispering that we had better consider all eventualities, without saying what they might be. But you had the courage to name them. You said, If we are separated, we shall meet again after the war. At home. Your last words.

. . .

We were separated. A stifled cry. A heartbeat. And our family was dispersed. Dislocated. When was it that we left the train? Discovered the barbed wire? When was it that the order came: "Families, stay together!" In a fraction of a second I was no longer the same. The uprooting was total, definitive: a sense of loss, of abandonment. I kept looking for you in the crowd, I kept looking for you to call you, to follow you, to tell you the things a son must say to his mother and I would no longer be able to say. Ever since, I feel stifled.

Yet I did see you.

But we were apart. And you did not turn back.

I saw you in front of me.

Is that true? But in front of you the night was in flames.

I saw you.

I only saw your back, I saw you only from the back.

. . .

I am still looking for you. The war is over and I want to go home. But I no longer have a home. They separated us and we did not meet again.

. . .

But I go on looking for you, I try to stop the tide. I see you walking hand in hand with my little sister. I see you both and there is a knot in my throat and it gets tighter and tighter. I ache. I ache and I don't know how to keep myself from howling. I ache and I don't know what to say, what to do.

Pilgrimage to
the Kingdom of Night

THE BEGINNING, the end: all the world's roads, all the outcries of mankind, lead to this accursed place. Here is the kingdom of night, where God's face is hidden and a flaming sky becomes a graveyard for a vanished people.

The beauty of the landscape around Birkenau is like a slap in the face: the low clouds, the dense forest, the calm solemnity of the scenery. The silence is peaceful, soothing. Dante understood nothing. Hell is a setting whose serene splendor takes the breath away.

A fluke of nature, or was it planned by the torturers? This contrast between God's creation and human cruelty is to be found wherever the Nazis implemented their Final Solution: Here, as at Treblinka, Maidanek, and Buchenwald, the theoreticians and technicians of collective horror carried out their work surrounded by beauty, not ugliness.

Only now do I discover the harmony and beauty of Birkenau. Surely, I was not aware of it thirty-five years ago. Then I saw only barbed wire; it bounded the universe. Sky? Birkenau had no sky. Only today do I perceive its blinding and searing light; it consumes memory.

When was this spellbound spot most unreal—in 1944 or today? I look at the watchtowers, the alleyways of the camp, and suddenly, as in a dream, they are filled with people. Once again I am confronting the fearful and faceless creatures of the past; they move in a world apart, a time apart, beyond life and death.

And once again I hear the tumult of the convoy disembarking in the night. Harsh shouting, stifled crying, soft moans and the barking of dogs. The efficient machinery kills thought before it crushes life. Where are we? Where are we going? Auschwitz: never heard of it. Birkenau: never heard of it.

The red flames that lick the sky inspire neither fear nor memory. The barbed wire stretches away into infinity, and the child in me says, "Ah, so that's what infinity is like!" Transmitted by a thousand lips, a simple order is all it takes to divide the crowd: men to one side, women to the other. Last words, last looks. In the human flood that flows slowly by, I see for the last time a mother and her small daughter, eerily silent and withdrawn. I see them moving forward, holding hands as if to reassure each other. I will see them that way, walking away from me, to the end of my life.

As in the past, I hear someone reciting the Kaddish. Who can it be? A dead man? A survivor? Have we, since that first night in the death camps, said or done anything but recite the prayer of the dying for the dead? Have we lived other than in their dreams? Then why does the sun shine so brightly? Here, at Birkenau, the sun shines in the middle of the night. Is that why I returned? To make this discovery? No. Survivors do not come back to Birkenau. They have never left.

This is why, for such a long time, I resisted coming back. And then, too, I was afraid. Afraid of the ghosts I would meet—and afraid of not meeting them. Afraid to recognize myself among them, afraid of not recognizing myself. More than anything else, I was afraid of finding myself in a museum.

Someday, I told myself, someday I'll make the trip. I'll take my son and his mother, and together we will make this pilgrimage. I will show them the place: look, look well; here mankind's hopes were transformed into darkness. I will show them the altar of ashes that has laid its curse upon our century. Someday, someday.

The day came both sooner and later—and certainly differently—than I had expected. I would never have imagined that I might one day come to Birkenau accompanied by reporters and television cameras. Such a trip should be made but once, and alone.

There were forty-four of us in the delegation, sent by the President's Commission on the Holocaust to visit the former death camps in Poland and the execution sites in Russia. Jews and Christians, young and old, survivors and friends, we had been charged by President Carter with the mission to recommend an appropriate program for remembering the victims of the Holocaust.

We were never alone. And yet each of us had never been so alone. These men and women, these survivors, remembered those they had lost as they stood at the very sites where they had disappeared. One had to be there in order to understand that there are some kinds of loneliness that can never be overcome. Only those who lived through the Event know what it was; the others will never know.

Loneliness is the key word that evokes, that describes the Jewish experience during World War II. Up and down streets and alleys within the Warsaw ghetto six hundred thousand Jews endured hunger and terror before they succumbed.

Why didn't the Polish population protect them— or at least help them? We tried, Polish officials tell us. They quote facts and figures. A hundred thousand Jews managed to hide. . . . An underground organization was formed for the sole purpose of rescuing Jews. . . . Perhaps. But the few who succeeded in escaping from the *Umschlagplatz*, where the Jews were assembled to be herded into the cattle cars, and from the death trains themselves, were unable to find shelter anywhere; they were forced to return to the ghetto. And the fact remains that when the ghetto—during and after the insurrection—burned for days and nights, many inhabitants of the capital came to enjoy the spectacle of Jewish freedom fighters jumping into the flames. The fact remains that today there are six thousand Jews in Poland. Before the war, there were three million five hundred thousand.

It is only natural, therefore, that a Jew feels out of place in today's Poland. He looks for his brothers and he fails to find them; even among the dead. A sentence here, a line of verse there, an allusion: not enough to recall their memory to future generations. We all suffered, Polish officials tell us; we lost three million non-Jewish Polish citizens, too. . . .

High-level meetings, discussions, ceremonies. The scenario is everywhere the same. The hosts refer to victims in general; we speak of Jews. They mention all the victims, of every nationality, of every religion, and they refer to them en masse. We object: of course, they must all be remembered, but why mix them anonymously together? Both Poles and Jews must be remembered, but as Poles *and* as Jews. The Jews were murdered because they were Jews, not because they were Poles. True, they both faced the same enemy; both were victims of the Nazis. But the Jews were victims of the victims as well. They, and they alone, were destined for total extermination, not because of what they had said or done or possessed, but because of what they *were*; to ignore this distinction, this essential fact about them, is to deny them. And so we told our Polish hosts, If you forget the Jews, you will eventually forget the others.

This problem—how to reconcile the specifically Jewish victims with the universality of all victims—haunted us throughout our pilgrimage. In fact, it had begun long before. The uniqueness of the Holocaust was debated during many commission meetings. What about the Gypsies? And the Slavs? And what about the Armenians? As if one tragedy were exclusive of the other. As if, by speaking of Jews, we were somehow turning our backs on the millions of non-Jews the Nazis slaughtered. Which, of course, is not the case. Quite the contrary: as we evoke the Jewish martyrdom, we also recall the sufferings and deaths of the non-Jewish victims. The universality of the Holocaust must be realized in its uniqueness. Remove the Jews from the Holocaust, and the Event loses its mystery.

As the meetings in Poland went on—with the Minister of Justice, the First Deputy Foreign Minister, high officials of the Ministry for War Veterans—our hosts began to show more and more understanding, and that is to their credit. They understood that many Jews see Poland as one immense and invisible cemetery, the vastest in all history.

On the eve of *Tisha B'av*, the day commemorating the destruction of the Temple in Jerusalem, we went to Warsaw's only remaining synagogue, on Nozyk Street. We were welcomed by a dozen congregants, including two American rabbis. The service was held in a small, dilapidated side room, as the main synagogue was being repaired.

Following custom, we turned the benches upside down and, by candlelight, began to recite the *Eicha*, the Lamentations of Jeremiah: "How doth the city sit solitary, that was full of people?"

As I read aloud the Prophet's evocation of a desolate Jerusalem, I stole a look at the "Jewish community" of Warsaw: a few haggard old people. And I was struck by the incongruity of the situation: the text was referring to Jerusalem, but it applied to Warsaw, to Jewish Warsaw. In our day, Jerusalem is very much alive, filled with exuberance: its sons and daughters shout their faith and joy to the world. Jeremiah is speaking about Warsaw and its dead or exiled Jews. What is left of Warsaw, its Talmudic schools, its cultural clubs, its Hasidic centers, its political groups, its sages and its princes? A small Jewish theater, a few offices, a Yiddish weekly.

The Jews of Warsaw are no longer in Warsaw; they are in Treblinka, two hours away.

THE JEWS of Warsaw are beneath the stones of Treblinka; they are the stones of Treblinka.

There they stand at attention, silently accusing.

Everyone knows about Treblinka. To mislead the victims, their murderers built a fake railroad station with fake signs and a clock set permanently at 6 P.M. It was all fake. Only death was real, voracious, waiting. When the Jews awoke to the fact that their end was near, it was too late. They were already being herded into the gas chambers; they were already being shoved in together; they were already dying.

The best description of Treblinka comes from Yankiel Wiernik, a carpenter. He knew the camp, he saw what no man can see without losing his mind, and he bore witness. His fifty-page testament, written and published in 1944, still keeps me awake at night.

The victims' tears, the sneering of their executioners, the funeral pyres, the dead children, the desperate attempts of sick prisoners to look "happy" because the S.S. sergeant loathed unhappy, weak, sick people and sent them off to die. . . . As I touch the stones of Treblinka, I think of Yankiel Wiernik. I think of him and of his comrades when, in an unprecedented surge of anger and futile bravery, they turned against their killers and fought back. Their armed uprising will remain one of the great events in the history of the war. Most of those who got away perished as "free men" at the hands of the Germans and their Polish accomplices. How can the memory of their struggle be kept alive? Here, the courage of the rebels and the resignation of the masses go hand in hand:

they cannot be separated. All were worthy and equal in the face of death.

The hundreds upon hundreds of stones that cover the length and breadth of Treblinka illustrate this equality: all of them, large and small, are impregnated with the same silence. From afar, in the twilight, they can easily be mistaken for Jews at prayer, wrapped in their ritual shawls.

People come from all over to look at the stones. They come to question them: How was it possible? We shall never understand. Even if we manage somehow to learn every aspect of that insane project, we will never understand it: How could human beings have done *that* to other human beings?

In the midst of the nightmare, Yankiel Wiernik wondered, too: What is the meaning of this slaughter? What brought it about? And why, why is it taking place? He could not understand. Nor can I. I think I must have read all the books—memoirs, documents, scholarly essays and testimonies—written on the subject. I understand it less and less.

I prefer the stones of Treblinka.

AUSCHWITZ is another matter. It is a kind of museum, and that is how it is listed on our schedule: Auschwitz, a museum. Clean, well-kept, a real museum. There are photographs, maps, arrows on the walls to direct us. The guides explain: This way, ladies and

gentlemen. The gate swings open. Here is the courtyard. Here are the watchtowers, the S.S. barracks, the
offices. This way to the bunker, a jail within the jail,
this way to the crematorium. . . . We are led from
one block to another, we are taken to visit the recently
completed Jewish pavilion, we are shown the wall
against which saboteurs and runaways were shot.

The whole place is unreal, less stirring than Treblinka. In order to see anything, I am forced to shut
my eyes. Block 17: I was here. This is where I lived.
I seek out my father's friends, my ageless, nameless
companions. A shout. They run outdoors and I run
after them. Here, everything is done on the double.
You run to wash up, to go to bed, to fall out for roll
call. Slow, deliberate steps are for the German over-
lords, not for their slaves. I reopen my eyes. This way
to the cafeteria.

Auschwitz souvenirs, Auschwitz postcards. . . .
This tourist attraction has a strange effect on former
inmates. It's the old story: To attract a large public,
you have to use a language it can understand. Some
concessions are necessary, perhaps even permissible,
if the end is a good one—and is there a higher purpose
than that of recalling the crimes against the Jewish
people and humanity that were committed here?
When obscene propagandists are publishing books to
"prove" that Treblinka and Auschwitz never existed,
what can be more urgent than attracting as many
visitors as possible to the place that was Auschwitz,

where every building is still intact, open for examination by the skeptical? So be it then, visit the museum—as long as it remains unaltered, authentic.

And yet . . . how can one describe the horror of a victim, any victim, at "selection" time, when his or her name may be called? How can hunger be depicted, obsessive hunger; how can it be conveyed? In more general terms: Can the era of Auschwitz be communicated to another era? A hard question. On a factual level, of course, the museum achieves an important result. Visiting it we know at least that there was a time when, in these very barracks, men from different countries and backgrounds were subjected to the same law and confronted the same darkness. In Auschwitz, at least, you know that Auschwitz really existed.

To learn more—to feel more—go to Birkenau.

WITHOUT A WORD being spoken, the survivors of Birkenau withdraw from other members of the delegation and form a separate group. They take each other's arms and walk slowly to the ramp, they cross the tracks, and they do not stop until they come to the ruins of the gas chambers and the crematorium. (The open pits nearby—where are they? Do I still see the flames?) Standing there, each withdraws into himself to shut out the present.

At that moment, it became important to erase

all the years, all the words, all the images that separated us from this event, from this place; it became
essential to rediscover night in all its nakedness and
truth; we had to recapture the unknown before it
could become known.

I heard the wind rushing through the trees, but
it was not really the wind. I heard the murmur rising
from the earth, but it was not the earth that spoke. It
was night. It was death.

What hasn't been said about this place? Philosophers and historians, psychologists and novelists,
dramatists and filmmakers, explorers of the human
soul and the unconscious, moved by honest emotions
or practical considerations, have all found in this universe of ashes a subject to be investigated, and rightly
so: no subject is more vital to our generation. To understand its deepest concerns, one must only connect
them with the phenomenon of Birkenau. The anger
of the young, the weariness of their parents, their common religious or quasi-religious yearnings for abso-
lutes, all these things are rooted here. And yet . . .
words, even the most profound, the most human
words, mean little here. In the past, in the universe of
barbed wire, force was all that counted. And yet . . .
and yet.

I stood alongside the former inmates of Birkenau
and Auschwitz, at the place where we had lost our
families, and I did not know what to say.

There was nothing to say.

Terrified Jewish children, stubborn Gypsies, the resigned old people and the sick, living dead brought from the four corners of Christian and enlightened Europe perished here. No, there were no words.

A prayer, then? Which one? There is no prayer in any book for such places. Only the victims had the right, and perhaps the strength, to pray. But there was no one there to hear them.

No one? Yes, no one. Except for members of the *Sonderkommando*, those desperate and tragic inmates who were forced by the killers to incinerate the corpses before they themselves were burned. They saw and heard everything. And they were determined to testify. Their diaries were recovered from beneath mountains of ashes. Leib Langfus, Zalmen Leventhal, Zalmen Gradowsky: these ill-fated chroniclers related the victims' final moments. Some had screamed, others had meditated, still others had cursed their killers, and there were those who had prayed to the God of Israel to remain faithful to the people of Israel.

No, for us there was nothing to say. But suddenly, inexplicably, a cry arose. The cry was ours and it reverberated in the wind, the cry of Jewish martyrs since the beginning: *Shma Israel*. "Hear, O Israel, God is our God, God is one." After a long silence, we withdrew, slowly stepping backward; we were shivering. Behind us a man began to chant softly, *Ani maamin*. "I believe with all my heart in the coming of the Messiah. . . ."

Surely he will come some day. We all believe it. But it will be too late.

THE RETURN to Birkenau was the high point of our pilgrimage, which did not lack dramatic moments. Some were moving, others disappointing. Our visit to Babi Yar, on the outskirts of Kiev in the Soviet Union, was both.

I had been there before, in 1965. At that time, there was no monument to the Jewish victims. Naturally I had protested. In my book on Russian Jewry, *The Jews of Silence*, an entire chapter is devoted to Babi Yar, the ravine where, over the course of ten days beginning on September 29, 1941, close to one hundred thousand Jews were massacred by the Nazis and buried in mass graves.

Now, as a result of pressure from abroad, there is a monument at Babi Yar. It is majestic, grandiose, like all the monuments in Soviet Russia. But . . . nowhere does there appear the word "Jew."

Though sensitive to all that relates to the Nazi era, officials turned a deaf ear to our complaints. The Mayor of Kiev and his aides, the Deputy Minister for Culture, Soviet Prosecutor General Roman A. Rudenko (who served as Russian Prosecutor General at Nuremberg), and officials of the Writers' Union all offered the same answer: In our country, we make no distinction between Jews and non-Jews.

The same discussions occurred as in Poland, the same arguments. The same pleas: Do not erase the Jewishness of the Jewish victims. The Christian members of the delegation—Bayard Rustin, Robert McAfee Brown, Franklin Littell, Alice and Roy Eckardt—never missed an opportunity to lend us their support. Publicly, at receptions, and privately we pleaded our case. In vain. The Russians simply refused to understand our point of view, our concerns, our fears that if the Soviet line were to prevail, history would be distorted and forgotten in one generation or two.

RUSSIAN JEWS want to remain Jews—a fact that no one dreams of denying anymore. I witnessed this during my trips to the Soviet Union in 1965 and 1966. In those days, the Jewish renaissance was still clandestine. Except on the Simhat Torah holiday, when thousands of young people gathered before the great synagogue in Moscow to sing and dance and to celebrate their faith, one saw nothing but fear on Jewish faces. Since then, things have changed. The doors have opened: hundreds of thousands of Jews have left the Soviet Union for Israel and the United States, and the flow is increasing.

Aspiring emigrants demonstrate extraordinary courage. Their leaders wished to meet with us. We visited their homes, we listened. They ask for little, only not to have to wait more than five years for their exit visas.

Alerted only the evening before, hundreds of Moscow Jews came eagerly to the Moscow synagogue to greet their American visitors. The hall was packed. The service was solemn and joyous. On this "Sabbath of Consolation," a chapter of Isaiah is read: "Comfort ye, comfort ye my people." This time the chapter was meaningful on a more immediate level, too: Russian and American Jews found in one another reason to hope.

I had received permission to address the congregation from the pulpit; never has a speaker had a better audience. As in the 1960s, men and women urged us, Don't forget us, please don't forget us! An old man looked at me and a glimmer of recognition lit up his wrinkled face. "I remember you," he said as he embraced me. "You have not forgotten us." I smiled. Never has a messenger been so rewarded.

The most welcome guest, however, was a young boy called Elisha who had come with us from the United States. The Moscow Jews could not stop admiring him, caressing his hair and kissing his hands longingly, as though he were a prince from a faraway land. It had been years since they had seen a little Jewish boy saying his prayers in their synagogue.

I thought of my father. The Russian soldiers could have saved him. But they arrived late, too late— for us. We had already been marched off to Gleiwitz, and from there, in open cattle cars, to Buchenwald. We were surrounded by corpses; we no longer knew

who was alive and who was not. I remember a man—
my father—murmuring to himself, or to the icy wind
that lashed his face: "What a pity, what a pity. . . ."
Did he regret not having tried to stay behind? Did
he feel sorry for those of us who were to survive? I remember another man shouting crazily. Others recited
the last confession. Still others chanted prayers for
Yom Kippur. The collective hysteria lasted for days
and nights, for years and lives.

And there is nothing left to say. Another Kaddish? And another one? How many prayers can one
say for an entire world? How many candles must one
light for mankind? So as not to betray ourselves by
betraying the dead, we can only open ourselves to
their silenced memories.

And listen.

Sighet Again

For most Americans, the name Transylvania evokes a country haunted by Dracula. For me, who was born there, it means something entirely different. In fact, I never learned of the existence, or rather the legend, of that malevolent count, one whose bizarre habits could not help but make him a star of Broadway and Hollywood, until after my arrival in the United States. When asked about my birthplace, I would naively reply that I came from a little city deep in a forgotten province called Transylvania, and no one would let me say more before the laughter started. The laughter would grow all the heartier because I understood nothing of it. "Ah, Dracula," they would say, with a wink. All right: now I know.

Yet you should not think that the Jewish children of Transylvania lived happily and without fear. They lived happily, but not without fear. We were always worried, anxious, threatened from all sides. Bandits, we were told, were spying on us from high in the mountains. And there were the louts and cowards, steeped in some ancestral hatred, who would attack us and beat us; like Dracula, they apparently needed to draw some blood—Jewish blood—to feel proud of themselves.

I am no longer a child, but even today Transylvania still chills me, or rather, a little corner of Transylvania does: Sighet, my native city. I live there no longer, yet it lives within me. It has been forty years since I left there for good, yet I am still a little fearful each time I see the place again. If I were a tourist seeking that perfect place to spend a holiday, to learn a little and to relax as well, I would go there without hesitation.

Why not, after all? Easily reachable, picturesque and inexpensive, Sighet has everything you could want: mountains, rivers, hotels, and memories.

You would take the plane or a train from Bucharest to Baia Mare, in Maramures, and from there a bus or a cab would take you to the other side of the mountain, into a valley. Yet another twisting road climbs over Satu Mare, wandering through villages, small towns and hamlets so bright and colorful and yet so apparently untouched by time, so nearly primitive, that they seem to belong to an earlier age.

Here, peasants look as they do in picture books, dressed as they have been through the ages, representing today as always that durable connection with their livelihood: the earth, trees, animals, flowers, the sky. For them, official communism is but an abstraction, and like their parents they feel most at home in church.

SIGHET, my birthplace, is a little city, so much like any other and so little like any other. Except for a few new apartment buildings, the houses are the same ones I used to pass on my way to school or on my way to my grandmother's.

Back then, before the torment, it was a little Jewish city, a typical *shtetl*, rambunctious and vibrant with beauty and faith, with its yeshivas and its workshops, its madmen and its princes, its silent beggars and noisy big shots. We spoke Yiddish among ourselves, responded to others in Romanian or Hungarian or Ruthenian, and we prayed in Hebrew. In the Jewish streets the businessmen argued in the morning and made up by evening; in the *shtiblech* the Hasidim said their prayers, studied the Midrash, told wonderful stories about their miracle-working rabbis.

Immersed in Jewish life, following the rhythms of the Hebrew calendar, the city rested on the Sabbath, fasted on the Day of Atonement, danced on the eve of Simhat Torah. Even the Christians knew there was no point in asking for bread in a Jewish bakery during Passover week, and that you should never offer to buy a glass of Tzuica for a Jewish bartender on the ninth day of the month of Av, for that day, marked by mourning, recalls the destruction of the Temple at Jerusalem.

All that is now gone. The Jews of my city are now forgotten, erased from its memory. Before, there were some thirty synagogues in Sighet; today, only one survives. The Jewish tailors, the Jewish cobblers, the Jewish watchmakers have vanished without a trace, and strangers have taken their place.

IT HAS BEEN twenty years since I first returned. Maybe it was just out of simple curiosity. Others like me have done so. The young and the no longer young return to the scenes of their youth, to the ruins of their past. Some want to perform the ancient ritual of praying at the graves of their ancestors. Others just want to see their own homes, their yards, their neighbors. There was a time when they were the only tourists here.

So it was twenty years ago that I first revisited these streets, walking for hours on end. I still remember: Passersby saw me without seeing, and I saw them while beholding only the ghosts that surrounded them, and the ghosts were more real, more vivid than they. I saw friends long dead, comrades long dead, dead rabbis, dead disciples, and they were alive. I had planned on staying a few days but fled after only a few hours.

The second time, I returned with a television crew working on a documentary. It was impossible to go anywhere alone, and, always accompanied, always under surveillance, I felt like an actor in an unsettling role. As soon as the filming was done, I turned my back once again on my city.

Now I am here on my third visit. I was invited by the Romanian-Jewish community, and I joined its chief rabbi, Dr. David-Moses Rosen, in a melancholy pilgrimage to commemorate the deportation of Transylvania's Jews forty years ago.

For four days, all of them superbly and efficiently organized by the authorities, we went from one city to the next, from one ceremony to the next: Dej, Satu Mare, Oradea, Sarmas: How many ceremonies does it take to mark the deaths of thousands and thousands of men, women, and children? How many times must one say *el Molé Rachamim*, the Prayer of Compassion? From everywhere, it seemed, moved by a mysterious call, Jews came out of their towns near and far, came to weep together, to plumb that collective memory from which their brothers and parents, beyond a desert of ashes, spoke to them, speak to them.

At Sighet I visited the Jewish cemetery where lies the grave of the grandfather whose name I bear. It was strange: I felt more at home among the graves than among the living beyond the gate. An extraordinary serenity dwelt in the graveyard, and I spoke quietly to my grandfather and told him what I have done with his name.

Then, with a childhood friend, a fellow pilgrim, we ambled through the streets and alleys in silence, not daring to glance at one another. I recognized each window, each tree. Names and faces sprang before me as if from nowhere, as if preparing to reoccupy their former homes. I stopped before my old house, and with a beating heart, nearly beside myself, I waited for a youth to come out to call me closer, to demand to know what I was doing there in his life. A nameless anguish came over me: What if all that I had lived had only been a dream?

IN THE SPACE of six weeks a vibrant and creative community had been condemned first to isolation, then to misery, and finally to deportation and death.

The last transport left the station on a Sunday morning. It was hot, we were thirsty. It was less than three weeks before the Allies' invasion of Normandy. Why did we allow ourselves to be taken? We could have fled, hidden ourselves in the mountains or in the villages. The ghetto was not very well guarded: A mass escape would have had every chance of success. But we did not know.

Hear me well, those of you who want to spend your vacation somewhere in Transylvania: You will not meet my friends there. They were massacred because no one thought it was necessary to warn them, to tell them not to go quietly into those windowless train cars. If this tragedy of Transylvanian Judaism hurts, if it hurts so terribly, it is not only because its victims are so near to me but also because it could have been prevented: Had the Allies moved faster and their leaders protested louder, many lives would have been saved.

So, you understand, the beauty of the countryside, the serenity and comfort and the hospitality that awaits the visitor, none of that is for me. But go, if it tempts you. And why wouldn't Transylvania tempt you? Despite the barely concealed police state, despite the poverty, you may be happy there. The gardens are splendid, the hotels are new, the reception that awaits you is warm.

Only, while you explore the cities and the villages, while you enjoy their special picturesqueness, try to evoke within yourself the memories of the men and women, and the children—especially the children—who forty years ago were driven away from this place and who today travel endlessly through mankind's wounded memory, signaling us invisibly, and yet so needfully, for the sake of our own survival.

Kaddish in Cambodia

ON THE EIGHTEENTH DAY (in the Hebrew calendar) of Shevat I found myself in the dusty, noisy village of Aranyaprathet, on the border between Cambodia and Thailand, searching desperately for nine more Jews.

I had Yahrzeit for my father, and I needed a *minyan* so that I could say Kaddish. I would have found a *minyan* easily enough in Bangkok. There are about fifty Jewish families in the community there, plus twenty Israeli Embassy families, so there would have been no problem about finding ten men for *minchah*. But in Aranyaprathet?

I had gone there to take part in a March for the Survival of Cambodia organized by the International Rescue Committee and Doctors Without Frontiers. There were philosophers, novelists, parliamentarians, and journalists—myriad journalists. But how was I to find out who might be able to help me with *my* problem?

I would have liked to telephone one of my rabbi friends in New York or Jerusalem and ask his advice on the Halakhic aspects of the matter. What did one do in such a case? Should one observe the Yahrzeit the following day, or the following week? But I was afraid of being rebuked and of being asked why I had gone to Thailand precisely on that day, when I should have been in synagogue.

I would have justified myself by saying that I had simply been unable to refuse. How could I refuse when so many men and women were dying of hunger and disease?

I had seen on television what the Cambodian refugees looked like when they arrived in Thailand—walking skeletons with somber eyes, crazy with fear. I had seen a mother carrying her dead child, and I had seen creatures dragging themselves along the ground, resigned to never again being able to stand upright.

How could a Jew like myself, with experiences and memories like mine, stay at home and not go to the aid of an entire people? Some will say to me, Yes, but when you needed help, nobody came forward. True, but it is *because* nobody came forward to help me that I felt it my duty to help these victims.

As a Jew I felt the need to tell these despairing men and women that we understood them; that we shared their pain; that we understood their distress because we remembered a time when we as Jews confronted total indifference. . . .

Of course, there is no comparison. The event which left its mark on my generation defies analogy. Those who talk about "Auschwitz in Asia" and the "Cambodian Holocaust" do not know what they are talking about. Auschwitz can and should serve as a frame of reference, but that is all.

So there I was in Thailand, in Aranyaprathet, with a group of men and women of good will seeking to feed, heal, save Cambodians—while I strove to get a *minyan* together because, of all the days of the year, the eighteenth day of Shevat is the one that is most full of meaning and dark memories for me.

Rabbi Marc Tanenbaum was a member of the American delegation. Now I needed only eight more. Leo Cherne, the president of the International Rescue Committee, was there as well. Only seven more to find.

Then I spotted the well-known Soviet dissident, Alexander Ginsburg, and rushed over to him. Would he agree to help me make up a *minyan*? He looked at me uncomprehendingly. He must have thought I was mad. A *minyan*? What is a *minyan*? I explained: a religious service. Now he surely did not understand. A religious service? Here, by the mined bridge separating Thailand and Cambodia? Right in the middle of a demonstration of international solidarity? I began all over again to explain the significance of a *minyan*. But in vain. Alexander Ginsburg is not a Jew; he is a convert to the Russian Orthodox Church. I still had seven to find.

Suddenly, I caught sight of the young French philosopher Bernard-Henri Levy, who was making a statement for television. Only six more to find. Farther on, I found the French novelist Guy Suares. Then a doctor from Toulouse joined us, followed by Henry Kamm, of *The New York Times*. Another doctor came over. At last there were ten of us. There, in the midst of all the commotion, a few yards from the Cambodian frontier, we recited the customary prayers, and I intoned Kaddish, my voice trembling.

Then, suddenly, from somewhere behind me, came the voice of a man still young, repeating the words after me, blessing and glorifying the Master of the Universe. He had tears in his eyes, that young Jew. "For whom are you saying Kaddish?" I asked him. "For your father?" "No." "For your mother?" "No."

He grew reflective and looked toward the frontier. "It is for them," he said.

Making the Ghosts Speak

HAVE I CHANGED? Of course. Everyone changes. To live means to traverse a certain time, a certain space: with a little luck, some traces of life are left. Those at the beginning are not the same as those at the end. Of course, my tradition teaches me that the road always leads somewhere, and although the destination remains the same, at different stages of the journey we change and renew ourselves. Drawn to childhood, the old man will seek it in a thousand different ways.

I AM SEEKING my childhood; I will always be seeking it. I need it. It is necessary for me as a point of reference, as a refuge. It represents for me a world that no longer exists; a sunny and mysterious place where beggars were princes in disguise, and fools were wise men freed from their constraints.

At that time, in that universe, everything seemed simple. People were born and died, hoped and despaired, understood certain things—not everything. I resigned myself to the idea that the quest is itself a victory; even if it hardly succeeds, it represents a triumph. It was enough for me to know that someone knew the answer; what I myself sought was the question.

It was in this way that I viewed man and his place in creation: it was up to him to question what surrounded him and thus to go beyond himself. It is not by chance, I told myself, that the first question in the Bible is that which God puts to Adam: "Where are you?"

"What?" cried a great Hasidic Master, Rabbi Shneour-Zalmen of Ladi. "God didn't know where Adam was? No, that's not the way to understand the question. God knew, Adam didn't."

That, I thought, is what one must always seek to know: one's role in society, one's place in history. It is one's duty to ask every day, "Where am I in relation to God and to others?"

And, strangely enough, the child knew what the adult did not. Yes, in my small town somewhere in the Carpathian Mountains, I knew where I was. I knew why I existed. I existed to glorify God and to sanctify his word. I existed to link my destiny to that of my people, and the destiny of my people to that of humanity. I existed to do good and to combat evil, to accomplish the will of heaven; in short, to fit each of my acts, each of my dreams, each of my prayers into God's design.

I knew that God was at the same time near and far, magnanimous and severe, rigorous and merciful. I knew that I belonged to his chosen people—people chosen to serve him by suffering as well as by hope. I knew that I was in exile and that the exile was total, universal, even cosmic. I knew as well that the exile would not last, that it would end in redemption. I knew so many things, about so many subjects. I knew especially when to rejoice and when to lament: I consulted the calendar; everything was there.

Now I no longer know anything.

As in a dusty mirror, I look at my childhood and I wonder if it is mine. I don't recognize myself in the child who studies there with fervor, who says his prayers. It's because he is surrounded by other children; he walks like them, with them, head bowed and lips firm. He advances into the night as if attracted by its shadows. I watch them as they enter an abyss of flames, I see them transformed into ashes, I hear their cries turn into silence, and I no longer know anything, I no longer understand anything: they have taken away my certainties, and no one will give them back to me.

IT'S NOT ONLY a matter of questions concerning religious faith. It's a matter of those, and all others. It's a matter of redefining, or at least rethinking, my relations with others and with myself: have they changed? I think that I can answer Yes without the slightest hesitation. My attitude toward Christians, for example: before the war, it was mistrustful, if not hostile; after, it became more open and hospitable.

Before the war, I avoided everyone who came from the other side—that is, from Christianity. Priests frightened me. I avoided them; so as not to pass near them, I would cross the street. I dreaded all contact with them. I feared being kidnapped by them and baptized by force. I had heard so many rumors, so many stories of this type; I had the impression that I was always in danger.

At school I sat with Christian boys of my age, but we didn't speak to one another. At recess we played separated by an invisible wall. I never visited a Christian schoolmate at his home. We had nothing in common. Later, as an adolescent, I stayed away from them. I knew them to be capable of anything: of beating me, humiliating me by pulling my *payess* or seizing my *yarmulke*, without which I felt naked. My dream back then? To live in a Jewish world, completely Jewish, a world where Christians would have scarcely any access. A protected world, ordered according to the laws of Sinai. It's strange, but awakening in the ghetto comforted me: after all, we were living among our own. I didn't yet know that it was only a step, the first, toward a small railroad station somewhere in Poland called Auschwitz.

But the deepest change took place not in the camps, but after their liberation. During the ordeal, I lived in expectation: of a miracle, or death. Atrophied, I evolved passively, accepting events without questioning them. Certainly, I felt revulsion toward the murderers and their accomplices, and anger toward the Creator who let them act as they did. I thought that humanity was lost forever and that God himself was not capable of saving it. I asked myself questions which formerly would have made me tremble: about the evil in man, about the silence of God. But I continued to act as though I still believed. Friendship in the camp was important to me; I looked for it despite the efforts of the killers to belittle and deny it. I clung to family ties despite the killers who changed them into dangerous, even fatal traps. As for God, I continued to say my prayers.

IT WAS ONLY later, after the nightmare, that I underwent a crisis, painful and anguished, questioning all my beliefs.

I began to despair of humanity and God; I considered them both enemies of the Jewish people. I didn't express this aloud, not even in my notes. I studied history, philosophy, psychology; I wanted to understand. The more I learned, the less I understood.

I was angry at the Germans: How could they have counted Goethe and Bach as their own and at the same time massacred countless Jewish children? I was angry at their Hungarian, Polish, Ukrainian, French, and Dutch accomplices: How could they, in the name of a perverse ideology, have turned against their Jewish neighbors to the point of pillaging their houses and denouncing them? I was angry at Pope Pius XII: How could he have kept silent? I was angry at the heads of the Allied countries: How could they have given Hitler the impression that, as far as the Jews were concerned, he could do as he wished? Why hadn't they taken action to save them? Why had they closed all doors to them? Why hadn't they bombed the railroad line to Birkenau, if only to show Himmler that the Allies were not indifferent?

And—why not admit it?—I was angry at God too, at the God of Abraham, Isaac, and Jacob: How could He have abandoned His people just at the moment when they needed Him? How could He have delivered them to the killers? How could one explain, how could one justify, the death of a million Jewish children?

For months and months, for years, I lived alone. I mistrusted my fellow humans; I no longer believed in the word as a vehicle of thought and of life; I shunned love, aspiring only to silence and madness. Disgusted with the West, I turned toward the East. I was attracted by Hindu mysticism; I was interested in Sufism; I even began to explore the occult domains of marginal sects here and there in Europe. I was anxious to venture to the other side of reality, of what constituted the basis of reality. Meditation counted more for me than action; I drowned myself in contemplation. The appearance of things repelled me, that of people even more.

If I had been able to settle in an ashram somewhere in India, I would have. But I couldn't. I had seen, under the incandescent sky of India, an immeasurable, unnameable suffering. I couldn't bear it. In the face of this suffering, the problem of evil imposed itself on me with a destructive force. I could choose to steel myself against it or flee. I was not anxious to be an accomplice. Hindu friends would cross the street stepping over mutilated and sick bodies without even looking at them. I couldn't. I looked and I felt guilty.

Finally I understood: I am free to choose my suffering but not that of my fellow humans. Not to see the hungry before me was to accept their destiny in their place, in their name, for them and even against them. Not to notice their distress was to acquiesce to its logic, indeed to its justice. Not to cry out against their misery was to make it all the heavier. Because I felt myself too weak to cry out, to offer a hand to so many disfigured children, because I refused to understand that certain situations couldn't be changed, I preferred to go away. I returned to the West and its necessary ambiguities.

After this, I practiced asceticism in my own way: in my home, in my little world in Paris, where I cut myself off from the city and from life for weeks on end. I lived in a room much like a prison cell—large enough for only one. The street noises that reached me were muffled. My horizon became smaller and smaller: I looked only at the Seine; I no longer saw the sky mirrored in it. I drew away from people. No relationship, no liaison came to interrupt my solitude. I lived only in books, where my memory tried to rejoin a more immense and ordered memory. And the more I remembered, the more I felt excluded and alone.

I felt like a stranger. I had lost my faith, and thus, my sense of belonging and orientation. My faith in life was covered with ashes; my faith in humanity was laughable; my faith in God was shaken. Things and words had lost their meaning. An image of the Kabbala described the state of my soul at that time: all of creation had moved from its center in order to exile itself. Whom was I to lean on? What was I to cling to? I was looking for myself, I was fleeing from myself, and always there was this taste of failure, this feeling of defeat inside me.

A member of the *Sonderkommando* of Treblinka asked himself if one day he would laugh again; another, of Birkenau, wondered if one day he would cry again.

I didn't laugh, I didn't cry. I was silent, and I

knew that never would I know how to translate the silence that I carried within myself; again I found myself in the ghetto.

In a sense I am still there. It's natural. I can do nothing about it: the ghetto is in me, in us. It will never leave us. We are its prisoners.

AND YET, there has been a change in our behavior. First of all, we express ourselves. I force myself to share the secret that consumes me. I try to make the ghosts within me speak. Does that mean that the wound has healed over? It still burns. I still cannot speak of it. But I can *speak*—that's the change.

A need for communication? For community perhaps? I evoke memories that precede my own; I sing the song of ancient kingdoms; I describe swallowed-up worlds. I exist by what I say as much as by what I hold back. To protect my silent universe, I speak of the world of others. To avoid painful subjects, I explore others: Biblical, Talmudic, Hasidic, or contemporary. I evoke Abraham and Isaac so as not to reveal the mystery of my relationship with my father. I recount the adventures of the Besht so as not to dwell on the fate of his descendants. In other words, literature has helped me look away. The tales that I recount are never those that I would like to tell, or ought to tell.

The problem is that the essential will never be said or understood. Perhaps I should express my thought more clearly: it's not because I don't speak that you won't understand me; it's because you won't understand me that I don't speak.

That's the problem, and we can do nothing about it: the life certain people have lived, you, the reader, will never live—happily for you, moreover. Their experience has set them apart: they are neither better nor worse, but different, more vulnerable and at the same time stronger than you. The least slight wounds them, but death does not frighten them. You look at them askance, and they suffer from your look; and yet, they know how to take the hardest blows, the worst disappointments.

This is true for both their relationship with the rest of humanity and their relationship with God. From God they await everything, and yet they are aware that everything will scarcely suffice. God Himself cannot change the past; even He cannot negate the fact that the killer has killed six million times. How could man redeem himself? I don't know. I suppose that he cannot.

THIS IS what I thought after the war; this is what I still think. And yet, I am surprised to feel a forgotten need to recite certain prayers, to sing certain melodies, to plunge into a certain atmosphere that defined my adolescence. Like most survivors, I would give everything I own to awaken and see that we are in 1938–1939; that I had only dreamed the future.

I would give much to be able to relive a Sabbath in my small town. The whiteness of the tablecloths, the flickering candlelight, the beaming faces around me, the melodious voice of my grandfather, the Hasid of Wizhnitz, inviting the angels of the Sabbath to accompany him to our home: I ache when I think of these things.

That is what I miss most: a certain peace, a certain melancholy that the Sabbath, at Sighet, offered its celebrants, big and small, young and old, rich and poor. It is this Sabbath that I miss. Its absence recalls to me all else that is gone. It reminds me that things have changed in the world, that the world itself has changed. And I have, too.

Passover

"THIS IS THE BREAD of affliction which our forefathers ate in the land of Egypt. Let all who are hungry enter and eat thereof. . . ."

Thus begins the Seder, that ancient family ceremony in which from time immemorial all Jews everywhere can and should relive an event that took place thirty-five centuries ago.

Like all Jewish children, I loved this holiday more than any other. Both solemn and joyous, it allowed us an escape from time. Slave of the pharaoh, I followed Moses into the unknown, into the desert, into death. His summons to freedom was stronger than fear.

The Seder transformed our very being. On that evening, my father enjoyed the sovereignty of a king. My mother, softer and lovelier than ever, seemed a queen. And we, the children, were all princes. Even visitors—the travelers and forsaken beggars we'd invited to share our meal—acted like messengers bearing secrets, or like princes in disguise.

How could I not love Passover? The holiday began well before the ceremony itself. For weeks we lived in a state of anticipation filled with endless preparations.

The house had to be cleaned, the books removed to the courtyard for dusting. The rabbi's disciples assisted in making the matzoh. Passover meant the end of winter, the victory of spring, the triumph of childhood.

HERE I MUST interrupt my reverie, for I see that I'm using the past tense. Is it because none of this is true anymore? Not at all. The meaning of the festival and its rites has scarcely changed at all. But everything else has.

I still follow the rituals, of course. I recite the prayers, I chant the appropriate Psalms, I tell the story of the Exodus, I answer the questions my son asks. But in the deepest part of myself, I know it's not the same. It's not as it used to be.

Nothing is. An abyss separates me from the child I once was. Today I know that no happiness can be complete. In fact, I'll go further and say that now, at this holiday time, the joy I should feel is tainted with melancholy.

It's understandable, of course. Passover was the last holiday I celebrated at home.

I RECALL all this in order to tell you why it's impossible for me to talk about Passover only in the present tense.

Do I love it less than before? No. Let's just say I love it differently. Now I love it for its questions, the questions which, after all, constitute its *raison d'être*.

The purpose of the Seder is to provoke children to ask questions. "Why is this night different from all other nights?" Because it reminds us of another night, so long ago, yet so near, the last night a persecuted and oppressed people, our people, spent in Egypt. "Why do we eat bitter herbs?" To remind us of the bitter tears that our forefathers shed in exile. Each song, each gesture, each cup of wine, each prayer, each silence is part of the evening's ritual. The goal is to arouse our curiosity by opening the doors of memory.

On this evening, all questions are not only permitted, but valid. And not only those which relate to the holiday. All questions are important; there is nothing worse than indifference. The story shows us four possible attitudes toward history: that of the wise son, who knows the question and asks it; that of the wicked son, who knows the question but refuses to ask it; that of the simple son, who knows the question but is indifferent to it; and finally, that of the ignorant son, who neither knows the question, nor is able to ask it.

In anguish, I wonder: What can we do not to forget the question? What can we do to vanquish oblivion?

WHAT SIGNIFICANCE does Passover have, if not to keep our memories alive? To be Jewish is to take up the burden of the past and include it in our concerns, our projects, and our obligations in the present.

We read the news and it's always the same: violence in Jerusalem, bombings in Lebanon, riots in Hebron. . . . Were it not for its past and its history, what right would Israel have? It is because of Moses, not only Sadat and Begin, that the peace between Israel and Egypt strikes one as miraculous.

As we recite the Haggadah, which tells us of the exodus of the children of Israel from Egypt, we experience a strange feeling, the feeling that we are living in Biblical times, living at a vertiginous pace.

My contemporaries have witnessed and lived through what no other generation has seen: the power of evil, but *also* the victory of a promise; the kingdom of night, but *also* the rebirth of a dream; Nazism and its victims, but *also* the end of the nightmare; the deaths at Babi Yar, but *also* the defiance of young Russian Jews, the first to challenge the Kremlin's police dictatorship.

Sometimes our heads spin, so frenzied and terrifying is the flow of events. History advances so quickly. And although man has conquered space, he has not conquered his own fears and prejudices. Have we learned nothing? All the wars that continue to rage, all the victims fallen to terrorists' bullets, all the children dying of hunger and disease in Africa and Asia. Why is there so much hatred in the world? And why so much indifference to suffering, to the anguish of others?

I love Passover because it remains for me a cry against insensitivity.

TWO STORIES. The first is about Job, who was in Egypt at the same time as Moses. What's more, he held the important position of adviser in the Pharaoh's court, with the same rank as Jethro and Bileam. When the Pharaoh asked how he might resolve the Jewish question, Jethro spoke in favor of Moses' request— to let his people go. Bileam, on the other hand, took the opposite stand. When Job was consulted, he refused to take sides; he wished to remain neutral, so he kept silent, neither for nor against. This neutrality, the Midrash says, earned him his future sufferings. At critical times, at moments of peril, no one has the right to abstain, to be prudent. When the life or death—or simply the well-being—of a community is at stake, neutrality is criminal, for it aids and abets the oppressor and not his victim.

The second story is no less provocative. It is found in the Midrash, in the passage about the Red Sea. The expected victims are saved at the eleventh hour, while their oppressors drown before their eyes. It is a moment of grace so extraordinary that the angels themselves begin to sing, but God interrupts them with the most humane, the most generous, the most sympathetic reminder. What has come over you? My creatures are perishing beneath the waves of the sea and you are singing? How can you praise me with your hymns while human beings die?

Although neither of these stories is part of the traditional Seder, I like to tell them. For me, Passover is an ongoing commitment to others and to compassion.

OH, I KNOW . . . it's easy enough to say. Compassion for the enemies of one's people—who has the right and the audacity to preach such a position? We can understand it on the level of God and the angels, but not on the human level. Why this story, then? To prompt us to question. If God demands compassion, then it must figure into the equation, it must play a role.

A topical question for the whole world—and for Israel and its inhabitants. Face to face with hatred, what should their attitude be? What do they feel, what should they feel, in the face of those Palestinians who treat them as despicable usurpers?

I have seen Israel at war, and I can attest to the fact that there was no hatred for enemy soldiers. Yes, there was a fierce desire and determination to win, but there was no hatred.

At the time, I remember how difficult it was for me to understand this phenomenon; it seemed illogical, irrational. For an enemy who desires only our destruction, you have to feel as much hatred as he feels for you. All of military history exists to prove it. But all of Jewish history exists to prove the contrary. The Jewish people have never had recourse to hatred, even when it involved a fight for survival.

If we'd had to hate all our enemies, we'd never have known where to stop.

And so, I return to the last holiday I celebrated at home with my family in my small town. The region was already infested with Germans. In Budapest, Adolf Eichmann was planning the deportation and liquidation of our communities. But we didn't know this. The Russian front seemed so close. At night we heard the cannons, we saw the reddening of the sky, and we thought: Soon, soon we will be free.

Communal prayer was forbidden in the synagogues, so we arranged to hold services in our house. Normally, on Passover eve, we chanted lightheartedly, enthusiastically. But not this time. This time we only murmured.

I remember now, and I'll always remember, that Seder. With bowed heads and heavy hearts, we evoked the old memories almost in silence; we dared not ask ourselves if, once again, God would intervene to save us.

In addition to my family, a strange visitor participated in the ceremony. In my imagination, I saw him as the Prophet Elijah. He spoke and fell silent and spoke again, like a madman. Fuming with rage, he frightened us with his cruel and horrifying stories.

Now I understand. He did not want to tell about the past but to predict the future. It is he too that I remember today when I invite "all who are hungry to come and eat." But he will not come. He will never come again. Nor will the others.

Meeting Again*

SOME THIRTY-SIX and thirty-seven years ago, we experienced, together, a moment of destiny without parallel—never to be measured, never to be repeated; a moment that stood on the other side of time, on the other side of existence.

When we first met, at the threshold of a universe struck by malediction, we spoke different languages, we were strangers to one another, we might as well have descended from different planets. And yet—a link was created among us, a bond was established. We became not only comrades, not only brothers; we became each other's witnesses.

I remember—I shall always remember the day I was liberated: April 11, 1945. Buchenwald. The ter-

* A speech delivered at the International Liberators Conference in Washington, D.C., on October 26, 1981.

rifying silence terminated by abrupt yelling. The first American soldiers. Their faces ashen. Their eyes—I shall never forget their eyes, your eyes. You looked and looked, you could not move your gaze away from us; it was as though you sought to alter reality with your eyes. They reflected astonishment, bewilderment, endless pain, and anger—yes, anger above all. Rarely have I seen such anger, such rage—contained, mute, yet ready to burst with frustration, humiliation, and utter helplessness. Then you broke down. You wept. You wept and wept uncontrollably, unashamedly; you were our children then, for we, the twelve-year-old, the sixteen-year-old boys and girls in Buchenwald and Theresienstadt and Mauthausen knew so much more than you about life and death. You wept; we could not. We had no more tears left; we had nothing left. In a way we were dead and we knew it. What did we feel? Only sadness.

And also: gratitude. And ultimately, it was gratitude that brought us back to normalcy and to society. Do you remember, friends? In Lublin and Dachau, Stuthoff and Nordhausen, Ravensbruck and Maidanek and Belsen and Auschwitz, you were surrounded by sick and wounded and hungry wretches, barely alive, pathetic in their futile attempts to touch you, to smile at you, to reassure you, to console you and most of all to carry you in triumph on their frail shoulders; You were heroes, our idols: tell me, friends, have you ever felt such love, such admiration?

One thing we did not do: We did not try to *explain*; explanations were neither needed nor possible. Liberators and survivors looked at one another—and what each of us experienced then, we shall try to recapture together, now, at this reunion which to me represents a miracle in itself.

At this point, allow me to say a few words about the Council whose chairman I am privileged to be.

Created by the President of the United States and unanimously enacted into law by both the U.S. Senate and the House of Representatives, our Council is essentially nonpolitical.

Our activities are manifold in nature and in scope. The International Relations Committee, which coordinated this conference, is but one of the committees functioning within the Council.

Moscow, 1979. Members of a Presidential delegation met with certain high-ranking Red Army officers. One of them in particular meant much to us: General Petrenko had liberated Auschwitz. It was an extraordinary encounter. We exchanged stories. He told us of the preparations to break through the German lines and I told him of the last day in camp, the last roll call, the last night, the last consultations among inmates, friends, fathers and sons. What should one do? Hide? Where? The Red Army was so near, so near. We prayed, I told General Petrenko. We prayed for you and your men and no believer ever prayed to his or her God with more fervor.

And so—while General Petrenko and I were telling each other tales of courage and despair, I suddenly had the idea of bringing together liberators from *all* the allied forces. To listen to you and to thank you. And—why not admit it?—to solicit your help. *Our* testimony is being disputed by morally deranged Nazis and Nazi-lovers; your voices may silence them. You were the first men to discover the abyss, just as we were its last inhabitants. What we symbolized to one another then was so special that it remained part of our very being.

Well—here you are, friends from so many nations, reunited with those who owe you their lives, just as you owe them the flame that scorched your memories.

On that most memorable day, the day of our liberation—whether it took place in 1944 or in 1945, in Poland or in Germany—you embodied for us humanity's noblest yearning to be free, and even more; to bring freedom to those who are not.

For us, you represented hope. True, six million Jews were annihilated, millions of brave men and women massacred by the Nazis and their collaborators, but we are duty-bound to remember always that to confront the fascist criminal conquests, a unique alliance of nations, gigantic armies, transcending geopolitical and ideological borders, was raised on five continents, and all went to war on behalf of humankind. The fact that millions of soldiers wearing different uniforms united to fight together, to be victorious together, and, alas, sometimes to die together, seemed to justify man's faith in his own humanity—in spite of the enemy. We thought of the killers and we were ready to give up on man; but then we remembered those who resisted them—on open battlefields as well as in the underground movements in France, Norway, Holland, Denmark, and the U.S.S.R.—and we reconciled ourselves with the human condition. We were—can you believe it?—naive enough to think that we who had witnessed, for a while, the domination of evil would prevent it from surfacing again. On the very ruins of civilization, we aspired to erect new sanctuaries for our children where life would be sanctified and not denigrated, compassion practiced, not ridiculed.

It would have been so easy to allow ourselves to slide into melancholic resignation. Instead we chose to become spokespersons for the human quest for generosity and need and capacity to turn suffering into something productive, something creative.

We had hoped then that out of so much grief and mourning a new message would be handed down to future generations, a warning against the inherent perils of discrimination, fanaticism, poverty, deprivation, ignorance, oppression, humiliation and injustice, and war—the ultimate injustice, the ultimate humiliation.

Yes, friends; we were naive.

And perhaps we still are.

Together we have the right and the duty to issue an appeal to which no one can remain deaf: an appeal against hatred, against human degradation, and against forgetfulness.

We have seen that which no one will ever see. We have seen what fanaticism leads to: mass cruelty, imprisonment, and death.

We have seen the metamorphosis of history, and now it is our duty to bear witness. When one people is destined to die, all others are implicated. When one ethnic group is humiliated, humanity is threatened. Hitler's plans to annihilate the Jewish people and to decimate the Slavic nations bore the germ of universal death. Jews were killed, but humankind was assassinated.

You, friends, liberators, stopped this process. Be proud. We are grateful.

If we unite our memories and wills, as we did then, everything is possible. Forgetfulness leads to indifference; indifference to complicity and thus to dishonor.

Friends, I speak to you as brothers. The ties that bind us to one another are powerful and timeless. Together we constitute a community that has no equal. Yet it diminishes from day to day. Who among you will be the last messenger? Our moral judgment, both past and present, determines our dignity. Yes, we are against prisons, against dictatorships, against fear, against confrontation, nuclear or otherwise. We give proof that it is possible for men and women to join forces and affirm the right to live and dream in peace.

I may be naive but I believe with all my heart that if we speak loudly enough, Death will retreat.

To paraphrase Nietzsche, we looked deep into the abyss—and the abyss looked back at us. No one comes close to the kingdom of night and goes away unscathed. We told the tale—or, at least, we tried. We resisted all temptations to isolate ourselves and be silent. Instead we chose to affirm our desperate faith in testimony. We forced ourselves to speak— however inadequately, however poorly. We may have used the wrong words—but then there are no words to describe the ineffable. We spoke in spite of language, in spite of the void that exists between what *we say* and outsiders *hear*. We spoke and . . . explosions in Paris, bombs in Antwerp, murderous attacks in Vienna. Is it conceivable that Nazism could dare come back into the open so soon—while we are still alive, while we are still here to denounce its poisonous nature, as illustrated in Treblinka?

Again we must admit our naiveté. We thought we had vanquished the beast, but no: it is still showing its claws. At best, what a gathering such as this could do is to shame the beast into hiding. If we here succeed—and I hope and pray that we shall—in rising above politics, above the usual recriminations between East and West, above simplistic propaganda, and simply tell the world what both liberators and liberated have seen, then something may happen; the world may choose to pay more attention to what hangs as a threat to its very future.

If we succeed—and I hope and pray that we shall—in putting aside what divides us—and what divides us is superficial—if we dedicate ourselves not only to the memory of those who have suffered but also to the future of those who are suffering today, we shall be serving notice on mankind that we shall never allow this earth to be made into a prison again, that we shall never allow war to be considered as a solution to any problem—for war *is* the problem. If we succeed, then our encounter will be recorded as yet another of our common victories.

If we do not raise our voices against war, against hate, against indifference—who will? We speak with the authority of men and women who have seen war; we know what it is. We have seen the burnt villages, the devastated cities, the deserted homes, we still see the demented mothers whose children are being massacred before their eyes, we still follow the endless nocturnal processions to the flames rising up to the seventh heaven—if not higher. . . .

We are gathered here to testify—together. Our tale is a tale of solitude and fear and anonymous death—but also of compassion, generosity, bravery, and solidarity. Together, you the liberators and we the survivors represent a commitment to memory whose intensity will remain. In its name we shall continue to voice our concerns and our hopes not for our own sake, but for the sake of humankind. Its very survival may depend on its ability and willingness to listen.

And to remember.

Trivializing Memory

WITTGENSTEIN SAID IT: Whereof one cannot speak, one must not speak. The unspeakable draws its force and its mystery from its own silence. A nineteenth-century Hasidic teacher put it his own way: The cry unuttered is the loudest.

If this is true of language as a means of communication in general, it is even truer of literature and art that try to describe, without ever succeeding, the final reality of the human condition during the Holocaust. Is proof needed? It has come in the recent spate of fictionalized accounts of that tragedy in the mass media.

Let us repeat it once again: Auschwitz is something else, always something else. It is a universe outside the universe, a creation that exists parallel to creation. Auschwitz lies on the other side of life and on the other side of death. There, one lives differently, one walks differently, one dreams differently. Auschwitz represents the negation of human progress and casts doubt on its validity. Then, it defeated culture; later, it defeated art, because just as no one could imagine Auschwitz before Auschwitz, no one can now retell Auschwitz after Auschwitz. The truth of Auschwitz remains hidden in its ashes. Only those who lived it in their flesh and in their minds can possibly transform their experience into knowledge. Others, despite their best intentions, can never do so.

Such, then, is the victory of the executioner; by raising his crimes to a level beyond the imagining and understanding of men, he planned to deprive his victims of any hope of sharing their monstrous meaning with others. In the tale of a survivor that appeared some twenty years ago, an S.S. officer tells a young Jew, "One day you will speak of all this, but your story will fall on deaf ears. Some will mock you, others will try to redeem themselves through you. You will cry out to the heavens and they will refuse to listen or to believe. . . ."

But not even the killers ever imagined that there could come a time when the merchants of images and the brokers of language would set themselves up to speak for the victims.

The Holocaust has become a fashionable subject, so film and theater producers and television networks have set out to exploit it, often in the most vulgar sense of the word. *The Night Porter, Seven Beauties,* the docudrama *Holocaust, Sophie's Choice,* and *War and Remembrance* (I speak of the films, not the books), *Murderers Among Us,* and the recent *Ghetto,* which played on Broadway for several weeks, and previously, to great acclaim, in Germany. These are only some of the most familiar examples over the years. An authentic documentary like *The Final Solution,* by the four-time Oscar winner Arthur Cohn, cannot find a distributor, but people fall all over themselves for cheap and simplistic melodramas. They get a little history, a heavy dose of sentimentality and suspense, a little eroticism, a few daring sex scenes, a dash of theological rumination about the silence of God, and there it is: let kitsch rule in the land of kitsch, where, at the expense of truth, what counts is the ratings.

WHY THIS determination to show "everything" in pictures? A word, a glance—silence itself communicates more and better. How, after all, can one illustrate famine, terror, the solitude of old people deprived of strength and orphans robbed of their future? How can one "stage" a convoy of uprooted deportees being sent into the unknown, or the liquidation of thousands and thousands of men, women, and children? How can one "produce" the machine-gunned, the gassed, the mutilated corpses, when the viewer knows that they are all actors, and that after the filming they will return to the hotel for a well-deserved bath and a meal? Sure, this is true of all subjects and of all films, but that is also the point: the Holocaust is not a subject like all the others. It imposes certain limits. There are techniques that one may not use, even if they are commercially effective. In order not to betray the dead and humiliate the living, this particular subject demands a special sensibility, a different approach, a rigor, strengthened by respect and reverence and, above all, faithfulness to memory.

You see, memory is more than isolated events, more even than the sum of those events. Facts pulled out of their context can be misleading. Take *Ghetto*. The author of this controversial production, Joshua Sobel, of Israel, insists that the play is based on fact. So what? By isolating certain facts, by giving them more prominence than so many others, and by illuminating them from a particular angle, he makes his play lie.

Ghetto is about a theater company in the Vilna ghetto that produced plays and concerts with the encouragement of Jacob Gens, the chief of the Jewish police, and the consent of the Germans. The author's intention? To show, on one hand, the will to live, the thirst for culture among Jews at the very threshold of death, and on the other, the moral ambiguity of some of their own leaders. It is a laudable idea, but the play shifts direction in mid-course.

What do spectators remember when they leave

the theater? The moral dilemma that faces Jacob Gens: May one sacrifice some human beings in order to save others? No. They remember the Jews, most of whom in this play allowed themselves to be defeated or seduced by the enemy. Bewildering scenes, nauseating in their collective degradation: orgies, depravity, sadistic exhibitionism, black-marketeering, prostitution, collaboration. With some notable exceptions, it is total decadence everywhere, debauchery and mockery at every level. Gens, a complex person, possesses astonishing dignity and courage, and yet he virtually becomes the Nazis' accomplice. His policemen become the Nazis' official instruments: it is they who hound the Jews, they who drive them to their deaths.

Is this a fair and true picture of the ghetto? Filmed as it is, full of ugliness, decadence, and moral abdication, it may be that it reflects a certain reality, but is that reality not a very limited one? It suffices to read the history of the Vilna ghetto, or to see a poignant film like *The Partisans of Vilna*, to realize how false and nasty a picture *Ghetto* paints for us. The religious vocabulary has a phrase for it: *Hilul hashem*—blasphemy or profanation, an act that strikes at all that is sacred.

WE ARE, in fact, living through a period of general desanctification of the Holocaust. In West Germany, historians are explaining away Hitler's crimes by lumping them with Stalin's; Chancellor Helmut Kohl's official spokesman recently said that Germans have had enough of feeling guilty and that the Warfen S. S. of Bitburg were only good German soldiers. In France, a man called Le Pen considers the Holocaust "a detail." Anti-Israeli propagandists compare Israeli soldiers to Nazis, and in France, as in the United States, and everywhere else, for that matter, shameless "revisionists" go so far as to deny the very existence of the death camps.

As for philosophers and psychiatrists, some of them have long been intrigued by simplistic theories that attribute to the victim a death wish or a secret need to dominate, to victimize, to oppress—in other words, to resemble the executioner. In the course of scholarly colloquia, one sometimes hears more about the guilt of the victims and the psychological problems of the survivors than about the crimes of the killers. Didn't an American novelist recently suggest that the suicide of my friend Primo Levi was nothing but a bout of depression that good psychoanalytical treatment could have cured? Thus is the tragedy of a great writer, a man who never ceased to battle the black angel of Auschwitz, reduced to a banal nervous breakdown.

Who could have imagined it? There are still living survivors, and already their past has been turned into a kind of no-man's-land where false certainties and arrogance rule. Newcomers to this history appoint themselves experts, the ignorant become critics. They give the impression of knowing better than the victims or the survivors how to name what Samuel Beckett called the unnameable, and how to communicate the uncommunicable. In the field of the audiovisual, the temptation is generally reductionist, shrinking personalities to stereotypes and dialogue to clichés. All is trivial and superficial, even death itself: there is no mystery in its mystery. It is stripped naked, just as the dead are stripped and exposed to the dubious enjoyment of spectators turned voyeurs.

Why this sudden explosion of nudity as a backdrop for the Holocaust? What by any rule of decency ought to remain unexposed is exposed to shock the television viewer. Naked men. Naked women. Naked children. And all of them made up with ketchup and paid to "fall" into the "mass graves." How can one explain such obscenity? How can anyone justify such insensitivity? In the Jewish tradition, death is a private, intimate matter, and we are forbidden to transform it into a spectacle. If that is true for an individual, it is six million times more true for one of the largest communities of the dead in history.

But then, the "experts" will ask, how do we transmit the message? There are other ways to do it, better ways to keep the memory alive. Today the question is not what to transmit, but how. Study the texts—such as the diaries of Emanuel Ringelblum and Chaim Kaplan; the works by the historians Raul Hilberg, Lucy Davidowicz, Martin Gilbert, Michael Marrus. Watch the documentaries, such as Alain Resnais's *Night and Fog*, Claude Lanzmann's *Shoah*, and Haim Gouri's *81st Blow*. Listen to the survivors and respect their wounded sensibility. Open yourselves to their scarred memories, and mingle your tears with theirs.

And stop insulting the dead.

Bitburg*

MR. PRESIDENT:

This medal is not mine alone. It belongs to all those who remember what S.S. killers have done to their victims.

It was given to me for my writings, teaching, and for my testimony. When I write, I feel my invisible teachers looking over my shoulders, reading my words and judging their veracity. While I feel responsible to the living, I feel equally responsible to the dead. Their memory dwells in my memory.

What have I learned in the last forty years? Small things. I learned the perils of language and those of silence. I learned that in extreme situations, when human lives and dignity are at stake, neutrality is a sin: it helps the killers, not the victims.

A speech delivered upon acceptance of the Congressional Gold Medal of Achievement at the White House, April 19, 1985.

I learned the meaning of solitude: we were alone—desperately alone. Leaders of the free world knew everything and did nothing—nothing specifically to save Jewish children from death. One million children perished. If I spent my entire life reciting their names, I would die before finishing the task. Children . . . I have seen some of them thrown into the flames . . . alive. Words? They die on my lips. I have learned the necessity of describing their deaths.

I have learned the fragility of the human condition. The killers were not monsters. They were human beings. Good parents. Obedient citizens. Some had college degrees and a passion for the arts or philosophy. Did their education prevent them from committing murder? Evidently not.

A great moral essayist, the gentle and forceful Abe Rosenthal, having visited Auschwitz, once wrote an extraordinary piece of reportage about the persecution of the Jews called "Forgive them not, Father, for they knew what they did."

I have learned that the Holocaust was a unique and uniquely Jewish event—albeit with universal implications. Not all victims were Jews; but all Jews were victims. Dachau's first inmates were German anti-Nazis; but Treblinka and Belzec and Ponar and Babi Yar were designed to serve as a sacrificial altar for the entire Jewish people.

I have learned the guilt of indifference. The opposite of love is not hate but indifference. Jews were killed by the enemy but betrayed by their so-called allies, who found political reasons to justify their indifference.

But I have also learned that suffering confers no privileges: it depends upon what one does with it. This is why survivors have tried to teach their contemporaries how to build on ruins. How to invent hope in a world that offers none. How to proclaim faith to a generation that has seen it shamed and mutilated.

THE SURVIVORS had every reason to despair of society; they did not. They opted to work for humankind, not against it.

A few days ago, on the anniversary of the liberation of Buchenwald, Americans watched with dismay as the Soviet Union and East Germany distorted both past and present history. Mr. President, I was there. I was there when American liberators arrived and gave us back our lives. What I felt for them will nourish me to the end of my life.

Mr. President, we are grateful to this country for having offered us haven and refuge. Grateful to its leadership for being friendly to Israel—for we are grateful to Israel for existing. Grateful to Congress for its continuing philosophy of humanism and compassion for the underprivileged. As for yourself, Mr. President, we are grateful to you for being a friend of the Jewish people, for trying to help the oppressed Jews in the

Soviet Union and for your continuing support of the Jewish State.

Mr. President, am I dreaming? Is this but a nightmare? This day was meant to be a day of joy for me, my family and our friends. Why then is there such sadness in my heart?

Allow me, Mr. President, to touch on a matter which is sensitive. I belong to a traumatized generation; to us symbols are important. Following our ancient tradition which commands us to "speak truth to power," may I speak to you of the recent events that have caused us much pain and anguish?

We have met four or five times. I know of your commitment to humanity. I am convinced that you were not aware of the presence of S. S. graves in the Bitburg cemetery. But now we all are aware of that presence. I therefore implore you, Mr. President, in the spirit of this moment that justifies so many others, tell us now that you will not go there: *that* place is not your place. Your place is with the *victims* of the S. S. We know there are political and even strategic considerations—but this issue, as all issues related to that awesome Event, transcends politics, and even diplomacy. The issue here is not politics but good and evil, and we must never confuse them. I have seen the S. S. at work; I have seen their victims.

There was a degree of suffering and loneliness in the concentration camps that defies imagination—cut off from the world, without refuge anywhere, sons watched helplessly as their fathers were beaten to death; mothers watched their children die of hunger. And then there was Mengele and his selections—terror, fear, isolation, and torture.

Mr. President, you seek reconciliation. So do I. I, too, wish to attain true reconciliation with the German people. I do not believe in collective guilt—nor in collective responsibility. Only the killers were guilty. Their sons and daughters are not. I believe we can, we must, work together with them and with all people to bring peace and understanding to a tormented world that is still awaiting redemption.

Testimony at
The Barbie Trial*

YOUR HONOR, gentlemen of the bench, gentlemen of
the jury, I thank you for inviting me to appear before
you today. I will try to speak about some of the nameless absent—but not for them. No one has a right to
speak in their name. If the dead have something to
say, they will say it in their own way. Perhaps they are
already saying it. Are we capable, are we worthy, of
hearing them?

May I say immediately that I feel no hatred toward the accused? I have never met him; our paths
have never crossed. But I have met killers who, like
him, along with him, chose to be enemies of my people and of humanity. I may have known one or another of his victims. I resembled them, just as they
resembled me: Within the kingdom of malediction

* Given in French in Lyon on June 2, 1987.

created by the accused and his comrades, all Jewish prisoners, all Jews, had the same face, the same eyes; all shared the same fate. Sometimes one has the impression the same Jew was being killed by the enemy everywhere six million times over.

No, there is no hatred in me: there never was any. There is no question of hatred here—only justice. And memory. We are trying to do justice to our memory.

Here is one memory: the spring of 1944. A few days before the Jewish Pentecostal holiday—*Shavuot*. This was forty-three years ago, almost to the day. I was fifteen and a half years old—my own son will turn fifteen in three days. A profoundly religious child, I was moved by messianic dreams and prayers. Far from Jerusalem, I lived for Jerusalem, and Jerusalem lived in me.

Though subjected to a fascist regime, the Jews of Hungary did not suffer too much. My parents ran a business, my three sisters went to school, the Sabbath enveloped us in its peace. . . . The war? It was nearing its end. The Allies were going to land in a day, in a week. The Red Army was twenty or thirty kilometers away. But then . . .

The Germans invaded Hungary on March 19, 1944. Starting then, events moved at a headlong pace that gave us no respite. A succession of anti-Semitic decrees and measures were passed: the prohibition of travel, confiscation of goods, wearing of yellow stars, ghettos, transports.

We watched as our world was systematically narrowed. For Jews, the country was limited to one town, the town to one neighborhood, the neighborhood to one street, the street to one room, the room to a sealed boxcar crossing the Polish countryside at night.

Like the forty-four Jewish children of Izieu (shipped to Auschwitz in 1944), the Jewish adolescents from my town arrived at the Auschwitz station one afternoon. What is this? we wondered. No one knew. The name did not evoke any memory in us. Shortly before midnight, the train began to move. A woman in our car began shouting, "I see a fire, I see a fire!" They made her be quiet. I remember the silence in the car. As I remember the rest. The barbed-wire fences stretching away to infinity. The shouts of the prisoners whose duty it was to "welcome" us, the gunshots fired by the S. S., the barking of their dogs. And up above us all, above the planet itself, immense flames rising toward the sky as though to consume it.

Since that night, I often look at the sky and see it in flames. . . . But that night, I could not look at the sky for long. I was too busy clinging to my family. An order rang out: "Line up by family." That's good, I thought, we will stay together. Only for a few minutes, however: "Men to the right, women to the left." The blows rained down on all sides. I was not able to say goodbye to my mother. Nor to my grandmother. I could not kiss my little sister. With my two older sisters, she was moving away, borne by the crazed, black tide. . . .

This was a separation that cut my life in half. I rarely speak of it, almost never. I cannot recall my mother or my little sister. With my eyes, I still look for them, I will always look for them. And yet I know . . . I know everything. No, not everything . . . one cannot know everything. I could imagine it, but I do not allow myself to. One must know when to stop. . . . My gaze stops at the threshold of the gas chambers. Even in thought, I refuse to violate the privacy of the victims at the moment of their death.

What I saw is enough for me. In a small wood somewhere in Birkenau I saw children being thrown into the flames alive by the S. S. Sometimes I curse my ability to see. It should have left me without ever returning. I should have remained with those little charred bodies. . . . Since that night, I have felt a profound, immense love for old people and children. Every old person recalls my grandfather, my grandmother, every child brings me close to my little sister, the sister of the dead Jewish children of Izieu. . . .

Night after night, I kept asking myself, What does all this mean? What is the sense of this murderous enterprise? It functioned perfectly. The killers killed, the victims died, the fire burned and an entire people thirsting for eternity turned to ash, annihilated by a nation which, until then, was considered to be the best educated, the most cultivated in the world. Graduates from the great universities, lovers of music and painting, doctors, lawyers, and philosophers participated in the Final Solution and became accomplices of death. Scholars and engineers invented more efficient methods for exterminating denser and denser masses in record time. . . . How was this possible?

I do not know the answer. In its scope, its ontological aspect, and its eschatological ambitions, this tragedy defies and exceeds all answers. If anyone claims to have found an answer, it can only be a false one. So much mourning, so much agony, so many deaths on one side, and a single answer on the other? One cannot understand Auschwitz either without God or with God. One cannot conceive of it in terms of man or of heaven. Why was there so much hatred in the enemy toward Jewish children and old people? Why this relentlessness against a people whose memory of suffering is the oldest in the world?

At the time, it seemed to me that the enemy's aim was to attack God Himself in order to drive Him from His celestial throne. Thus, the enemy was creating a society parallel to our society, a world opposed to ours, with its own madmen and princes, laws and customs, prophets and judges.

Yes, an accursed world where another language

was spoken, where a new religion was proclaimed: one of cruelty, dominated by the inhuman; a society that had evolved from the other side of society, from the other side of life, from the other side of death, perhaps; a world where one small piece of bread was worth all ideas, where an adolescent in uniform had absolute power over thousands of prisoners, where human beings seemed to belong to a different species, trembling before death, which had all the attributes of God. . . .

As a Jew, it is impossible for me not to stress the affliction of my people during their torment. Do not see this as an attempt to deny or minimize the sufferings of the populations of the occupied countries or the torture undergone by our comrades, our Christian or nonreligious friends whom the common enemy punished with unpardonable brutality. We feel affection and admiration for them. As though they were our brothers? They are our brothers.

It is impossible for me, as a Jew, not to stress that for the first time, an entire people—from the smallest to the largest, from the richest to the poorest—were condemned to annihilation. To uproot it, to extract it from history, to kill it in memory by killing all memory of it: such was the enemy's plan.

Marked, isolated, humiliated, beaten, starved, tortured, the Jew was handed over to the executioner, not for having proclaimed some truth, nor for having possessed envied riches and treasures, nor for having adopted a certain forbidden behavior. The Jew was condemned to death because he was born Jewish, because he carried in him a Jewish memory.

Declared to be less than a man, and therefore deserving neither compassion nor pity, the Jew was born only to die—just as the killer was born only to kill. Consequently, the killer did not feel in any way guilty. One American investigator formulated it this way: the killer had not lost his sense of morality, but his sense of reality. He thought he was doing good by ridding the earth of its Jewish "parasites."

Is this the reason Klaus Barbie, like Adolph Eichmann before him, does not feel guilty? Except for Höss, the commander of Auschwitz, condemned and hanged in Poland, no killer has repented. Their logic? There had to be executioners to eliminate a million and a half Jewish children; killers were *needed* to annihilate four and a half million Jewish adults.

Auschwitz and Treblinka, Maidanek and Ponar, Belzec and Mathausen, and so many others, so many other names: the apocalypse was everywhere. Everywhere, mute processions headed toward pits filled with dead bodies. Very few tears, very little crying. From their appearance, resigned, thoughtful, the victims seemed to be leaving the world without regret. It was as though these men and women were choosing not to live in a society disfigured, denatured by hatred and violence.

After the war, the survivor tried to tell about it,

bear witness . . . but who could find words to speak of the unspeakable?

The contemplative silence of old people who knew, of children who were afraid of knowing . . . the horror of mothers who had gone mad, the terrifying lucidity of mad people in a delirious world . . . the grave chant of a rabbi reciting the Kaddish, the murmur of his followers going after him to the very end, to heaven . . . the good little girl undressing her younger brother . . . telling him not to be afraid; no, one must not be afraid of death . . . perhaps she said, One must not be afraid of dead people. . . .

And in the city, the grand, ancient city of Kiev, that mother and her two children in front of some German soldiers who are laughing . . . they take one child from her and kill it before her eyes . . . then, they seize the second and kill it too. . . . She wants to die; the killers prefer her to remain alive but inhabited by death. . . . Then, she takes the two little bodies, hugs them against her chest and begins to dance . . . how can one describe that mother? How can one tell of her dance? In this tragedy, there is something that hurts beyond hurting—and I do not know what it is.

I know we must speak. I do not know how. Since this crime is absolute, all language is imperfect. Which is why there is such a feeling of powerlessness in the survivor. It was easier for him to imagine himself free in Auschwitz than it would be for a free man to imagine himself a prisoner in Auschwitz. That is the problem: no one who has not experienced the event will ever be able to understand it. And yet, the survivor is conscious of his duty to bear witness. To tell the tale. To protest every time any "revisionist," morally perverse as he may be, dares to deny the death of those who died. And the truthfulness of the memory transmitted by the survivors.

For the survivors, however, it is getting late. Their number is diminishing. They meet one another more and more often at funerals. Can one die more than once? Yes, one can. The survivor dies every time he rejoins, in his thoughts, the nightly procession he has never really left. How can he detach himself from them without betraying them? For a long time he talked to them, as I talk to my mother and my little sister: I still see them moving away under the fiery sky. . . . I ask them to forgive me for not following them. . . .

It is for the dead, but also for the survivors, and even more for their children—and yours—that this trial is important: it will weigh on the future. In the name of justice? In the name of memory. Justice without memory is an incomplete justice, false and unjust. To forget would be an absolute injustice in the same way that Auschwitz was the absolute crime. To forget would be the enemy's final triumph.

The fact is that the enemy kills twice—the second time in trying to obliterate the traces of his crime. That is why he pushed his outrageous, terrifying plan to the limits of language, and well beyond: to situate it out of reach, out of our range of perception. "Even if you survive, even if you tell, no one will believe you," an S. S. told a young Jew somewhere in Galicia.

This trial has already contradicted that killer. The witnesses have spoken; their truth has entered the awareness of humanity. Thanks to them, the Jewish children of Izieu will never be forgotten.

As guardians of their invisible graves, graves of ash encrusted in a sky of eternal night and fog, we must remain faithful to them. We must try. To refuse to speak, when speech is awaited, would be to acknowledge the ultimate triumph of despair.

"Do you seek fire?" said a great Hasidic rabbi. "Seek it in the ash." This is what you have been doing here since the beginning of this trial, this is what we have attempted to do since the Liberation. We have sought, in the ash, a truth to affirm—despite everything—man's dignity; it exists only in memory.

Thanks to this trial, the survivors have a justification for their survival. Their testimony counts, their memories will be part of the collective memory. Of course, nothing can bring the dead back to life. But because of the meetings that have taken place within these precincts, because of the words spoken, the accused will not be able to kill the dead again. If he had succeeded it would not have been his fault, but ours.

Though it takes place under the sign of justice, this trial must also honor memory.

When Memory Brings People Together*

ALLOW ME to read you a poem. It is in Yiddish:

> *Schtiler, schtiler, lomir schwajgn*
> *Kworim waksn do,*
> *s'hobn sej farflanzt di ssonim,*
> *Grinen sej zu blo.* . . .

> *Schtiler, kind majns, wejn nit, ojzer,*
> *s'helft nit kejn gewejn.*
> *Undser umglik weln ssonim*
> *Saj wi nit farschtejn.* . . .

> Hush, hush, let us be silent,
> Tombs are growing here.
> Planted by the enemy,
> They are green and turning blue. . . .

> Hush, my child, don't cry,

---

* *An address in the Reichstag, delivered on November 10, 1987.*

Crying won't do any good.
Never will the enemy
understand our plight. . . .

This lullaby was written in the ghetto by Shmelke Katchegirsky. Grieving Jewish mothers would chant it, trying to put their hungry and suffering children to sleep.

Tombs? These children—these innocent little children—were deprived of everything: their lives and even a burial place.

And so, hush, little children, one million of you, hush, come: we invite you. We invite you into our memory.

Yiddish in the Reichstag? There is significance in using this warm, melancholy, and compassionate language in a place where Jewish suffering and Jewish agony, some fifty years ago, aroused neither mercy nor compassion.

Yiddish was the tongue of many, if not most, of the Jewish victims who perished during the dark period when the Angel of Death seemed to have replaced God in too many hearts in this country. Yiddish too was their target and their victim.

There is significance, too—as there is irony and justice—in my speaking to you this afternoon from this very rostrum where my own death, and the death of my family, and the death of my friends, and the death of my teachers, and the death of my entire people were decreed by the legally elected leader of Germany. I would betray the dead were I not to remind you that his poisonous words did *not* make him unpopular with his people. Most applauded with fervor; some, very few, remained silent. Fewer still objected. How many Jews found shelter in how many German homes during the Kristallnacht? How many Germans tried to help extinguish the flames engulfing the synagogues? How many tried to save holy scrolls? How many cared?

In those days and nights humanity itself seemed to have been distorted and twisted in this city and nation which are proud of their distant history, but struggling with their recent memories. Everything human and divine was perverted then. The Law itself had become immoral. Here, in this city, in this place, it had become legal and commendable to humiliate Jews simply for being Jews and to hunt down children simply because they were Jewish children. It became legal and praiseworthy to imprison, shame, oppress, and, ultimately, destroy human beings—sons and daughters of an ancient people—because their very existence was considered a crime.

The official decision to implement the Final Solution was made at the highest level of German hierarchy, at a relatively brief but practical and congenial meeting that took place on January 20, 1942, in Wannsee.

The high officials who participated in the meet-

ing knew that they acted on behalf of their government and in the name of the German people, which
supported that government.

The atrocities committed under the law of the
Third Reich *must not* and *will not* be forgotten; nor
will they be forgiven. I said it when I was here nearly
two years ago: I have no right to forgive the killers for
having exterminated six million of my kinsmen. Only
the dead can forgive; and no one has the right to
speak on their behalf.

Still, not all citizens who were alive then were
guilty. As a Jew, I have never believed in collective
guilt. Only the guilty were guilty. Children of killers
are not killers, but children. I have neither the desire
nor the authority to judge today's generation for the
unspeakable crimes that were committed by that of
Hitler. But we may—and we must—hold it responsible,
not for the past, but for the way it remembers the past.
And for what it does with the memory of the past.

"Memory" is the key word. To remember is to
create links between past and present, between past and
future. To remember is to affirm man's faith in humanity and to convey meaning on our fleeting en-
deavors. The aim of memory is to restore its dignity
to justice.

It is in the name of memory that I address myself to Germany's youth. "Remember" is the commandment that dominates the life of young Jews to-

day; let it dominate yours as well. Challenged by memory, you could move forward. Opposed to memory, you are bound to remain eternally opposed to us and to all we stand for.

Memory means to live in more than one world, to be tolerant and understanding with one another, to accept the mystery inherent in questions and the suspicion linked to answers. Naturally, it can also bring forth tensions and conflicts, but they can then be transformed into culture, art, education, spiritual inquiry, the quest for truth, the quest for justice. Without memory, mankind's image of itself would be impoverished.

Of course, I understand—for you, it is not easy to remember. It may even be more difficult than it is for us as Jews. We try to remember the dead; you must remember those who killed them. Yes—there is pain involved in both attempts. Not the same pain. Open yourselves to yours, as we have opened ourselves to ours.

You find it hard to believe that your elders did those things? So do I. Think of the tormentors as I think of their victims. I remember every minute of their agony. I see them constantly. I am afraid: If I stop seeing them, they will die. I keep on seeing them, and they died nevertheless.

I remember: January 20, 1942, in my childhood town. It must have been a day like any other. Some

Jewish children were playing with snowmen, others studied hard at school. They were already dead here, in Berlin, and they did not know it.

There is something in all this I do not understand—and never will. Why such determination on the part of the killer to kill so many of my people? Why the old men and women? Why the children? Why an entire people? How was all that made possible?

You young men and women in Germany must ask yourselves similar questions—or the same questions.

A people that had produced Goethe and Schiller, Bach and Beethoven, had suddenly chosen to put its national genius in the service of evil and erect a monument named Auschwitz to its dark power.

A community that had contributed to culture and education, as few nations had, called culture and education into question. Now we know many killers had college degrees and were products of the best universities in Europe. Many came from distinguished families. I often wonder about the theological implications of Auschwitz, but here I must also recognize that Auschwitz was not sent down from heaven; Auschwitz was conceived, planned, constructed, managed, and justified by people. What human beings did there to other human beings will affect future generations. After Auschwitz, hope itself is filled with anguish.

But—after Auschwitz, hope is necessary. Where can it be found? In remembrance alone.

After the war, it took many Germans too long to

confront their past. Teachers did not teach, and pupils did not learn, the most tragic and important chapter in German history and world history. To confront it would be too painful, was the explanation. It took the Eichmann trial in Jerusalem for German courts to indict S. S. murderers who, after the war, quietly returned to their homes and resumed their trades—as if nothing had happened.

True, the situation in East Germany remains worse. Unlike the Federal Republic, which did make serious attempts under Konrad Adenauer to compensate survivors and help Israel, East Germany is hostile to Israel and refuses to pay reparations. East Germany, like Austria, behaves without the slightest trace of remorse.

The Federal Republic has chosen a more honest and enlightened course of action. You have succeeded, in a few decades, in creating a transition from brutal totalitarianism to true democracy. Individual freedom is respected. Your commitment to the Western alliance is strong.

Furthermore, there are among you individuals and groups who have been seeking atonement in word and in deed; some have gone to work for Israel, in Israel; others are involved in religious dialogues. Writers, artists, poets, novelists, statesmen: there are among them men and women who refuse to forget— and, make no mistake, the best books by German authors deal with the trauma of the past. . . .

Now, in the new Wannsee museum, you will show what was done to Jews, to Jews alone. You will show pictures of Jews before they died, you will show the cold brutality of those who killed them, you will show the passivity, the cowardly indifference of the bystanders.

However, in fairness, I feel I must point out negative elements in modern Germany: the extreme left is violently anti-Israel, the extreme right is anti-Jewish. Furthermore, it is bad enough that we have revisionists in our own countries—but must we encounter them in Germany too? I know: here it is illegal to publicly deny the Holocaust. Still, it is being done in a vulgar form—by neo-Nazis—and in a more subtle manner by some historians whose intent is to "normalize" and "relativize," and thus banalize, cheapen, and trivialize the most painful event in Jewish history. Their attitude is impudent, arrogant, obscene. Whether they want to or not, those historians will ultimately belong to the ugliest category of all—that of the revisionists who deny occurrence of the Holocaust; they serve the same gods. The normalization of the historians helps the revisionists in their fight against memory. Against the Jewish people.

But I wonder: "What has been the general response to the "Battle of the Historians"? I hope that you, young Germans, have taken part in it. I hope that you are, and will be, sensitive to Jewish pain. Was Bitburg really necessary? Was it essential for a Frankfurt theater to stage an anti-Semitic Fassbinder play? Was it a must for your government to show friendship toward an Austrian chancellor with whom the Jewish community at large was, and remains, in open conflict?

And how come the Bundesrat has never found it necessary to officially ask the Jewish people for forgiveness?

The United States Senate has recently adopted a bill that expresses an apology to the Nisai, the Japanese Americans who were imprisoned in 1941–1942. Why couldn't the German parliament offer a similar apology to the Jewish people? Germany would not be humiliated by such a move; just the opposite.

I appeal to you: Be our allies. Justify the faith we have in your future. Fight forgetfulness. Reject any attempt to cover up the past. Remember the Jewishness of the Jewish victims, remember the uniqueness of their tragedy. Thus, it is incumbent upon you not to allow the building of museums that do not distinguish between war casualties and victims of Nazism. Be the conscience of your nation. And remember: a conscience that does not speak up when injustices are being committed is betraying itself. A mute conscience is a false conscience.

Remember some lessons from your past and ours: Words can kill, just as they can heal. . . . Remember: It was possible to stop the machinery of death . . . to save lives. So few dared.

In remembering, you will help your own people to vanquish the ghosts that have been hovering over their history. Remember: a community that does not come to terms with the dead will find that the dead continue to perturb and traumatize the living. Reconciliation can be achieved through and in memory. Memory restores absence to presence and the dead to the living. Does it also involve pain? I welcome it. I think of the children—walking slowly, almost peacefully, toward the flames—and I am almost grateful for the pain that links me to them.

The children, the children: those of Lidice, those of Oradour, the Jewish children from all over occupied Europe who were handed over to the killers will forever haunt us with their silent pleas for a shred of kindness and consolation. Might they not have grown up to help mankind? Who knows? One of them might have discovered a cure for cancer or AIDS. In killing them, the killers and their accomplices punished themselves and the world.

Thus, in remembering them, we remember today's victims, too. We remember our hunger so as to eliminate starvation. We remember our anguish so as to proclaim the right of men and women everywhere to live without fear. We remember our death so as to denounce the insanity of violence and the absurdity, the ugliness, the shame of war.

We remember Auschwitz and all that it symbolizes because we believe that, in spite of the past and its horrors, the world is worthy of salvation; and salvation, like redemption, can be found only in memory.

So—here we are, back at my central obsession. But you may ask: Isn't there a danger that memory may perpetuate hatred? No, there is no such danger. Memory and hatred are incompatible, for hatred distorts memory. The reverse is true: memory may serve as a powerful remedy against hatred.

An example? At the end of the war, many Germans were afraid of Jews—they were afraid of Jews coming back for revenge. There was fear and trembling in German towns and villages. And the Jews could have come and unleashed retribution on a large scale—and nobody would have stopped them or even criticized them. But . . . it did not happen. Oh, I am not saying that there was no hatred in some Jews; there is a minority that hates Germany even today; its members do not buy German products, refuse to set foot on German soil, and refuse to acknowledge that young Germans are not guilty. One—a Jew born in Berlin—went so far as to urge me not to appear here today. . . .

But what I do maintain is that most Jews did not choose hatred as a response. Hatred is not a Jewish response and never has been. Nor is vengeance a Jewish response. The Jewish tradition understands that the punishment the killer most fears is the victim's memory of his deeds.

This is why the killer so wanted his crimes to be forgotten. This is why we must remember them.

We must remember them for the sake of our children. And yours. They all deserve from us an offering. An offering of hope.

For my generation, hope cannot be without sadness. Let the sadness contain hope, too.

More Dialogues

1. THE CHILD AND THE MOB

Why are you chasing me?
> *You are alone. We are against lonely children.*

And when I grow up, will you stop chasing me?
> *You won't grow up.*

Why not?
> *Something in you annoys us.*

What have I done?
> *Nothing. You have done nothing.*

But I don't even know you.
> *It's true, you don't know us.*

And you? Do you know me?
> *We don't know you.*

Then why do you chase me?
> *You bother us.*

And what if I promise to get out of your way?
> *You'll still bother us.*

What if I go into hiding?
> *You can't. We are everywhere.*

What if I promise not to look at you? To go blind?
> *The blind are dangerous; they see what we don't see.*

What if I die? Will I stop bothering you then?
> *You are clever. It's because you are clever that we are after you.*

What have you done to my father?
> *You are too young to know.*

What have you done to my mother?
> *You are too young to know.*

And my grandparents? What have you done to them?
> *They are old, too old for you to think of them.*

And my little sister, what happened to her?
> *You're really too curious for a boy of your age.*

Where is she? I love her.
> *Good for you.*

I promised to take care of her.
> *Good for you.*

Why have you separated us?
> *It's good for you.*

Are you happy when families are separated?

Very happy.

Then you are not human. You are . . . a wall.

A huge wall.

But walls come tumbling down.

Not ours. Ours climbs to the sky. And higher still.

It will come tumbling down, I'm telling you. You'll see. I know what I am saying. The wall that you have built on Jewish children. One day they'll move, and you'll fall down, all of you.

Nonsense. All Jewish children are dead.

They are dead, but they'll start moving, you'll see. And if I promise to forget you, will you let me go?

You could forget us?

Easy. All it takes is to think of something else, and finished: you're gone. The beautiful face of my grandfather, the heartbreaking expression on the face of my grandmother: I think of them, and you're but dust. You want to know something? You're weaker than the weakest Jewish child: we decide whether you exist or not.

You're joking.

Now listen: the joke is on you. It's true. You're laughing, but your laughter is false.

You dirty little Jew. You cast a spell on us! We can't laugh! Our throats have all dried up!

Not only your throats! Your minds also! And your

hearts! All dried up! You wake up only when you kill Jewish children!

You talk like a wise man, like an old man, like someone whose life is behind him. Like someone who is about to die.

Then you'll die with me. The moment my memory ceases to live, you're dead. In provoking my death, you justify your own.

Don't be insolent; you're in our hands; you're our prisoner!

I am in your hands, but you're our prisoners. In our memory, you're already dead. You're the dead prisoners of a living memory.

2. A MAN AND LANGUAGE

Why do you avoid me?

I am busy.

I need you.

Too bad. Look elsewhere.

Why are you hostile? Do you wish to hurt me?

Hurt is the wrong word; erase it from your vocabulary.

Why do you want me to erase words? I love words, don't you know that?

I merely asked you to erase one word.

Hurt?

Yes.

Why?

Because you have done the hurting.

Whom have I hurt?

Me. You spoke when you shouldn't have. You shouldn't have said anything.

Have I used forbidden words? Have I offended anyone? Have I blasphemed?

You are too concerned with people. You've forgotten me. You behaved as if I mattered little. And yet, what would you have done without me? How would you have communicated your memories through words and prayer? I am your link to the world. And still you have offended me.

But . . . by doing, by saying what?

You yielded to verbal temptation.

Should I have kept silent? And silenced the voices that incite me to rebellion?

Perhaps.

Then you would have been offended by my silence.

Perhaps.

And provoked as well?

Perhaps. But then, it's possible that I like being provoked. And that I also like silence—I mean the provocative kind.

I don't follow you.

You oppose me to silence, that's your mistake. The opposite of language is not silence but apathy. I get along rather well with silence. We couldn't live without each other.

And what is my role in all this?

Your task is to receive. Not to dominate. Your mistake was in wishing to do both. Instead of setting me free, you wanted to chain me. We are no longer allies.

But I love you! I have always loved you!

That's irrelevant.

But at least admit that you know how much I love you. You have traced the contours of my universe, the limits of my hope.

In that case, why have you sought to hurt me? An example? Do you remember when, in an unknown cemetery, you began looking for your father's grave?

I remember.

And yet, you knew that your father had no grave!

I knew.

And yet you went on looking.

What else could I have done? I am still looking for my father's grave, and will never cease to look for it everywhere.

Everywhere? Why not look inside you?

I am looking inside myself.

In other people too?

In them too.

In me?

Naturally . . .

See? I trapped you! I am nobody's grave! I can be memory or vision, but no grave! Each one of my words contains all the others. Each represents the beginning of a tale linked to the origins of creation. And you call me a grave?

There are graves filled with treasures. . . .

Real graves perhaps. But I was not created to be a grave. I was created to guide the living and help them overcome darkness.

I apologize.

You won't do it again?

I'll try.

What do you mean?

I'll try not to hurt you, but I shall continue to look for my father's grave. Don't you understand? The dead need graves. If my father had one, I would know what to do.

What would you do?

I would call him.

How? With tears? With words? Will you use me?

I don't know.

You have never called him?

I have. Often. Everything in me calls for him. But he doesn't answer. It's your fault. You stand between us.

Because of you he can't hear. Because of you he can't come near me.

Starting again?

Yes, starting again. The dead need cemeteries. At times, I imagine six million victims in search of graves, and I feel close to insanity.

Continue.

I begin to yell, and yet I say nothing. I shout but no sound is heard. Does that silence offend you?

My dear friend. Of all the words, your silence pleases me most. For there is a silence of the living and a silence of the dead. And I . . .

And you? You what?

3. AN OLD MAN AND DEATH

I am not scared of you.

Why do you say that?

I think you're the one to be scared.

You talk nonsense. Fear is a tool in my hands; I can direct it against anyone I wish. I rarely fail.

You'll fail now.

Your certainty borders on arrogance, old man.

I lived too long. So much so that if they try to send me back from heaven I'll say no.

Tired?

And how.

You wish to die?

I am too deeply rooted in my tradition to want to die. But I shall leave life without fear or regret.

You surprise me, old man, but I like you. A man your age who stands up to me like this, well, that's something. . . . Usually people kneel before me . . . and implore me to give them another year, another day. You should see them. . . .

You pitiless being. . . . First you humble them, then you despise them . . . you remind me of the enemy who, eternities ago, threw Jews in the mud and then insulted them for being dirty.

The enemy?

Your ally.

Because I deprive the living of their ability to live? Admit at least that I don't lack fairness. All fall before me. The good and the wicked. The killers who killed your parents, I will kill them, too. Can you imagine the world without me? God himself would lose his way. . . .

You are not God's messenger, but people's. Doesn't the Talmud call you "The messenger of people"?

The Talmud, the Talmud . . . it also claims that when God said "Tov meod"—Very good—he referred to me. Leave me alone with the Talmud.

Can you kill the Talmud?

No, but I have taken the lives of many Talmudic scholars.

Yet their word is more powerful than yours.

So what? In the end I win.

Always? Weren't you allowed to come near King David only when he recited Psalms?

A slight delay. Unimportant.

Obviously, you fail to understand. As long as we sing, you are powerless against us. Maybe that's why so many Jews, young and old, went to their death singing.

Are you proud of that?

Yes, I am. I am proud of all Jews who perished. Those who fought and those who prayed, I am their kinsman. Facing the executioner, facing you, they appeared human, sad but human, weakened but sovereign, starving but dignified.

You haven't seen them.

I have seen some.

Some wept like cowards.

Cowards? You said cowards? Because they wept? Are cowards the only ones to weep? Some people weep for noble reasons. You who remember humankind, have you seen that many orphaned parents, tortured children? Have you witnessed that many massacres?

Yes, I have.

You are lying.

You may say anything about me but that I am a liar. I never lie. I always tell the truth to those for whom I come. Yes, I have seen many massacres. That's my fate: nobody dies without my being present. My gaze kills. My breath creates mass graves. That's how it is, there is nothing I can do about it. I see them all and they all look alike. Alive, people intrigue me; dead, they bore me. All are equal before God? Before me too. Maybe I am God.

You are not.

How can you be that certain? God and I have many things in common. If He is the beginning, I am the end.

God participates, you don't.

But who writes the last word? I do.

No, you don't. All the catastrophes, the murders, the fires, they are all man's work, not yours.

But aren't men my emissaries? my accomplices? They do what I tell them to do—and undo.

It's nice of you to take responsibility for all the injustices and agonies in the world. But I refuse to place all the blame on you. For then the killers will not feel guilty. And the assassins will see themselves as victims. And the pogroms, the manhunts, the mountains of human ashes will be reduced to grandiloquent abstractions and solemn stupidities. Since our destiny is at stake, I refuse to judge you. But God will. As for us, human beings, we shall judge our fellow men and women in human terms alone.

You amuse me, old man. You talk, you talk and

with every word you come closer to me. And yet, you go on talking.

I'll be dead soon you're thinking? Well, beware: the dead may one day rise to slay you.

4.   A CHILD AND ANOTHER CHILD

Who are you?
I don't know.
Who am I?
I don't know.
Who knows?
The others. They know.
The others? Who are they?
The grownups.
What is a grownup?
Someone who gives orders, that's a grownup. Some-one scary who can kill us.
You mean the guards?
Yes. The guards.
They know who we are?
They know everything. They have prepared every-thing. That's what they are here for. To prepare every-thing. How many barracks, how many tents, how many bread rations. They must take care of us, see? After all, they won't throw us out like sick cats into

the garbage. A grownup is someone responsible, see what I mean?

No, I don't see.

> *What don't you see?*

How can they take care of us when they keep on saying that we are disgusting?

> *So what?*

So what? I'll tell you so what! If we are disgusting, they can throw us in the garbage.

> *If so, they'll need a huge garbage can, right? Do you know how many we are?*

I don't.

> *Can't you count?*

I can count.

> *Then start counting.*

I . . . I can't.

> *You forgot?*

I learned to count to ten. Maybe seventeen.

> *Ah, my poor fellow. Life doesn't stop at seventeen.*

What comes after seventeen?

> *Thirty. A hundred. A thousand.*

Are we a hundred children here?

> *More than a hundred.*

A thousand?

> *A thousand times a thousand.*

How many is that?

Many. We need a can as large as the whole planet, as deep as the ocean. Can you imagine the world as a gigantic garbage can?

The world?

Yes, the world. Created by God.

I can't believe it.

What can't you believe?

I can't believe that God Almighty would have worked so hard, first for six days, then for six thousand years, just to produce a cheap garbage can.

If you were He, what would you have produced?

A palace. A royal palace not only for kings, but for everybody. A palace that would transform all visitors into princes. And you?

If I were God?

If you were God, what would you do?

Things, simple things. First of all, I would order all cobblers to make shoes for all the children here. My feet hurt, see? And God should do something about my feet. And yours. And those of all the children. Look at us, we walk like invalids.

True. Like invalids. Barefoot invalids. My feet ache.

I am exhausted.

Not as much as me.

If I were God I would bring a huge forest and put it here, on the road before us. Then the transport would have to stop. And we could rest. I am sleepy, aren't you?

Sleepier than you.

If I were God I would see to it that all things would be sleepy. Trees. And stones. And trains. And guards.

That's all? I still prefer my royal palace. Except it isn't simple, I know that. If all people become princes, what about our guards? I don't want them to become princes. But . . . I think I have an idea. They will stay outside the palace gates. We'll call them only when we are cold: to light the fire in the stove.

But isn't it what they are doing now?

Now?

Yes, now. Look: the fire over there . . . The flames are as high as the heavens. They illuminate the world. . . .

No. Not the world; only the palace. I am so happy. God has granted my wish. My dream will be fulfilled. We are going to live in the most glorious palace in the world. And since God is so nice to us, we shall sing for Him, okay?

My body is aching. I can't sing.

We must. We'll dance, too. For Him. We want Him to be proud of us. And of all His creatures. Don't you agree that God is proud of us? I am proud of Him.

. . .

Do you hear me?
>   *I am listening.*

May I ask you a favor?
>   *Maybe.*

Teach me how to pray.
>   *I can't. I am too cold.*

Teach me . . . I don't want to freeze to death.
>   *Don't worry. We are approaching the palace.*

What Really
Makes Us Free?

Is THERE a nobler aspiration than the desire to be free? It is by his freedom that a man knows himself, by his sovereignty over his own life that a man measures himself. To violate that freedom, to flout that sovereignty, is to deny man the right to live his life, to take responsibility for himself with dignity.

Man, who was created in God's image, wants to be free as God is free: free to choose between good and evil, love and vengeance, life and death. All the great religions proclaim this. The first law after the Ten Commandments had to do with slavery: it prohibited not only owning slaves but also *entering into* slavery voluntarily. One who gave up his freedom was punished. To put it another way: Every man was free, but no man was free to give up his freedom.

To strip man of his freedom is not to believe in man. The dictator does not believe in man. Man's freedom frightens him. Imprisoned as much by his ambition as by his terror, the dictator defines his own freedom in relation to the lack of freedom of others. He feels free only because, and when, other people— his subjects, his victims—are not free. The happiness of others prevents him from being happy himself. Every free man is his adversary, every independent thought renders him impotent.

Caligula felt sure of his own intelligence only when faced with his counselors' stupidity; Stalin derived morbid pleasure from the humiliations he inflicted on his ministers; Hitler liked to insult his generals. Every dictator sees others as potential prisoners or victims—and every dictator ends by being his own prisoner and his own victim. For anyone who claims the right to deprive others of their right to freedom and happiness deprives himself of both. By putting his adversaries in prison, his entire country becomes one vast jail. And the jailer is no more free than his prisoners.

In fact, it is often the prisoner who is truly free. In a police state, the hunted man represents the ideal of freedom; the condemned man honors it. As Jean-Paul Sartre said, in Occupied France, the only free people were those in prison. These men and women rejected the comfort of submission and chose to resist the forces of oppression. Once imprisoned, tormented, tortured, they no longer had anything to fear. They knew they were lost.

When the great French Jewish humorist Tristan Bernard was arrested by the Germans after months in hiding, his fellow prisoners were surprised by his smiling face. "How can you smile?" they asked. "Until now, I have lived in fear," he said. "From now on, I shall live in hope."

It is because his victims cling to hope that the dictator persecutes them. It is because they believe in freedom as much as in life itself that he is determined to deprive them of both.

Heroes and martyrs became the pride of their people by fighting with a weapon in their hand or a prayer in their soul. In a thousand different ways, each proclaimed that freedom alone gives meaning to the life of an individual or a people.

For a people—that is, for a social, ethnic, or religious group—the problem and its solution are both simple. When a people loses its freedom, it has a right, a duty, to employ every possible means to win it back. But resistance can be expressed in nonviolent ways too.

The Jews who lived in the ghettos under the Nazi occupation showed their independence by leading an organized clandestine life. The teacher who taught the starving children was a free man. The nurse who secretly cared for the wounded, the ill, and the dying was a free woman. The rabbi who prayed, the disciple who studied, the father who gave his bread to his children, the children who risked their lives by leaving the ghetto at night in order to bring back to their parents a piece of bread or a few potatoes, the man who consoled his orphaned friend, the orphan who wept with a stranger for a stranger—these were human beings filled with an unquenchable thirst for freedom and dignity. The young people who dreamed of armed insurrection, the lovers who, a moment before they were separated, talked about their bright future together, the insane who wrote poems, the chroniclers who wrote down the day's events by the light of their flickering candles—all were free in the noblest sense of the word, though their prison walls seemed impassable and their executioners invincible.

It was the same even in the death camps. Defeated and downcast, overcome by fatigue and anguish, tormented and tortured day after day, hour after hour, even in their sleep, condemned to a slow but certain death, the prisoners nevertheless managed to carve out a patch of freedom for themselves. Every memory became a protest; every smile was a call to resist; every human act turned into a struggle against the torturer's philosophy.

Do not misunderstand me: I am in no way trying to minimize the Nazis' evil power. I am not saying that all prisoners succeeded in opposing them by their will to be free. On the contrary—locked in a suffering and solitude unlike any other, the prisoners generally could only adapt to their condition—and either be submerged by it or swept along by time. The apparatus of murder was too perfect not to crush people weakened by hunger, forced labor, and punishment. But I *am* saying that the executioner did not always triumph. Some victims managed to escape and alert the public in the free world. Others organized a solidarity movement within the inferno itself. One companion of mine in the camps gave the man next to him a spoonful of soup every day at work. Another would try to amuse us with stories. Yet another would urge us not to forget our names—one way, among many others, of saying No to the enemy, of showing that we *were* free, freer than the enemy.

Are We Afraid of Peace?

FROM TIME IMMEMORIAL, people have talked about peace without achieving it. Do we simply lack enough experience? Though we talk peace, we wage war. Sometimes we even wage war in the name of peace. Does that seem paradoxical? Well, war is not afraid of paradoxes.

Though temporary in nature, war seems to last forever. In the service of death, it mocks the living. It allows men to do things that in normal times they have no right to do: to indulge in cruelty. A collective as well as individual gratification of unconscious impulses, war may be too much a part of human behavior to be eliminated—ever.

Life on our planet would be so much easier if only men and nations could live in peace. But apparently they cannot. Is this because they are unaccustomed to it? Or perhaps because they need to simplify things? For war simplifies everything by reducing the options. The gulf separating good and evil widens. On one side, everything seems just; on the other, unjust. There is no need to think too hard about it—no one worries about subtleties in time of war. Time itself becomes subordinated to war.

If only we could celebrate peace as our various ancestors celebrated war; if only we could glorify peace as those before us, thirsting for adventure, glorified war; if only our sages and scholars together could resolve to infuse peace with the same energy and inspiration that others have put into war.

Why is war such an easy option? Why does peace remain such an elusive goal? We know statesmen skilled at waging war, but where are those dedicated enough to humanity to find a way to avoid war? Every nation has its prestigious military academies. Why are there no academies—or so few of them—that teach not only the virtues of peace but also the art of attaining it? I mean attaining and protecting it by means other than weapons, the tools of war. Why are we surprised whenever war recedes and yields to peace?

Unfortunately, we are forced to acknowledge that war seems inherent in the human condition—and in fact preceded it, according to an old Talmudic legend. Before God created man, says the Talmud, He was given contradictory advice by His angels. The Angel of

Love was in favor of creating man because he felt that in order to survive, men would have to love one another. But the Angel of Truth opposed this suggestion, because he knew that in order to exist in society, men would inevitably invent lies. As all the angels joined in the argument, it degenerated into a quarrel and then into open warfare. All but two—Michael and Gabriel, heavenly defenders of Israel—were destroyed by the fire that they themselves had lit.

Human beings turned out to be no better. Adam had scarcely been created before he quarreled with his wife and even with God. His two sons, Cain and Abel—the only children then on earth—became enemies and ultimately murderer and victim.

What lessons can be learned from this? Two men can be brothers and yet wish to kill each other; and also, whoever kills, kills his brother. But we only learn these lessons too late. In time of war, whoever is not our brother is our enemy; we are forbidden to be compassionate or give in to our imagination. If the soldier were to imagine the suffering he is about to inflict, he would be less eager to wage war. If he were to consider the enemy a potential victim—and therefore capable of weeping, of despairing, of dying—the relationship between them would change. Every effort is made, therefore, to limit, even stifle, his imagination, his humanitarian impulses, and his capacity to experience a feeling of brotherhood toward his fellow man.

Is this why people often appear so ill prepared for peace? As soon as peace knocks on the door, they seem paralyzed by distrust: what if it is but an illusion, a mirage, a trap? It is as though peace makes them uneasy—which is not unnatural, since we are so accustomed to living in fear of war that peace becomes a sort of elevated, remote ideal, something associated with the absolute, the transcendent. Peace has been so eagerly anticipated that its reality can only disconcert.

We are afraid to let ourselves go, to allow ourselves to be carried away by an enthusiasm born of wishful thinking. It is as though we cannot forget certain images and words which, only yesterday, characterized the other side as our adversary. How can we erase the collective memory of the Gulag atrocities, the occupation of Prague, the attack on Korea? How can we reconcile the terror of the KGB with *perestroika* and *glasnost*, Stalin's Kremlin with Gorbachev's?

Still, no matter how great the reward, we must not forget. There is no justification for forgetting. If we had to forget the past in order to obtain peace, I would say that I would want nothing to do with such a peace. It could only be a lie. It could only foster a costly and dangerous passivity.

What we must do is use our memory as an opening rather than a prison. What does our memory tell us? It tells us about the absurdity of territorial conquests today. Imperialism, whether political or ideological, is outmoded. Nothing is left of the empires of Napoleon or the czars. What remains of Stalin's global ambition? Communism is retreating everywhere. As for the Third Reich, which was to last a thousand years, today its name arouses horror and shame rather than admiration and envy.

In general, nationalism is less tied to geography than it used to be. Western Europe—for hundreds of years so fragmented and divided—is about to abolish its internal frontiers. Hereditary enemies such as France and England, France and Germany, will unite. Despite the past? Because of the past. Memory is a source of anguish, but it can also become a source of faith. And memory also reminds us that from now on war will be without glory. It will leave no conquerors, only victims.

J. Robert Oppenheimer expressed this aptly in his testimony before a Congressional committee in Washington. Asked what we had to do to avoid a nuclear war, he answered concisely: "Make peace."

The Nobel Address*

YOUR MAJESTY, Your Royal Highnesses, Your Excellencies, Chairman Aarvik, members of the Nobel Committee, ladies and gentlemen:

Words of gratitude. First to our common Creator. This is what the Jewish tradition commands us to do. On special occasions, one is duty bound to recite the following prayer: *Barukh shehekhyanu vekiymanu vehigianu lazman haze*—"Blessed be Thou for having sustained us until this day."

Then—thank you, Chairman Aarvik, for the depth of your eloquence. And for the generosity of your gesture. Thank you for building bridges between people and generations. Thank you, above all, for helping humankind make peace its most urgent and noble aspiration.

I am moved, deeply moved by your words, Chairman Aarvik. And it is with a profound sense of humility that I accept the honor—the highest there is—that

* Delivered on December 10, 1986, in Oslo, Norway, upon acceptance of the Nobel Prize for Peace.

you have chosen to bestow upon me. I know: your choice transcends my person.

Do I have the right to represent the multitudes who have perished? Do I have the right to accept this great honor on their behalf? I do not. No one may speak for the dead, no one may interpret their mutilated dreams and visions. And yet, I sense their presence. I always do—and at this moment more than ever. The presence of my parents, that of my little sister. The presence of my teachers, my friends, my companions. . . .

This honor belongs to all the survivors and their children and, through us, to the Jewish people with whose destiny I have always identified.

I remember: it happened yesterday or eternities ago. A young Jewish boy discovered the Kingdom of Night. I remember his bewilderment, I remember his anguish. It all happened so fast. The ghetto. The deportation. The sealed cattle car. The fiery altar upon which the history of our people and the future of mankind were meant to be sacrificed.

I remember he asked his father, "Can this be true? This is the twentieth century, not the Middle Ages. Who would allow such crimes to be committed? How could the world remain silent?"

And now the boy is turning to me. "Tell me," he asks, "what have you done with my future? What have you done with your life?" And I tell him that I have tried. That I have tried to keep memory alive, that I have tried to fight those who would forget. Because if we forget, we are guilty, we are accomplices.

And then I explain to him how naive we were—that the world did know and remained silent. And that is why I swore never to be silent whenever and wherever human beings endure suffering and humiliation. We must always take sides. Neutrality helps the oppressor, never the victim. Silence encourages the tormentor, never the tormented. Sometimes we must interfere. When human lives are endangered, when human dignity is in jeopardy, national borders and sensitivities become irrelevant. Wherever men or women are persecuted because of their race, religion, or political views, that place must—at that moment—become the center of the universe.

Of course, since I am a Jew profoundly rooted in my people's memory and tradition, my first response is to Jewish fears, Jewish needs, Jewish crises. For I belong to a traumatized generation, one that experienced the abandonment and solitude of our people. It would be unnatural for me not to make Jewish priorities my own: Israel, Soviet Jewry, Jews in Arab lands. . . . But others are important to me. Apartheid is, in my view, as abhorrent as anti-Semitism. To me, Andrei Sakharov's isolation is as much a disgrace as Josef Begun's imprisonment and Ida Nudel's exile. As is the denial of Solidarity and its leader Lech Walesa's right to dissent. And Nelson Mandela's interminable imprisonment.

There is so much injustice and suffering crying out for our attention: victims of hunger, of racism and political persecution—in Chile, for instance, or in Ethiopia—writers and poets, prisoners in so many lands governed by the Left and by the Right.

Human rights are being violated on every continent. More people are oppressed than free. How can one not be sensitive to their plight? Human suffering anywhere concerns men and women everywhere. That applies also to the Palestinians, to whose plight I am sensitive, but whose methods I deplore when they lead to violence. Violence is not the answer. Terrorism is the most dangerous of answers. They are frustrated, that is understandable; something must be done. The refugees and their misery; the children and their fears; the uprooted and their hopelessness: something must be done about their situation. Both the Jewish people and the Palestinian people have lost too many sons and daughters and have shed too much blood. This must stop, and all attempts to stop it must be encouraged. Israel will cooperate, I am sure of that. I trust Israel, for I have faith in the Jewish people. Let Israel be given a chance, let hatred and danger be removed from her horizons, and there will be peace in and around the Holy Land. Please understand my deep and total commitment to Israel: if you could remember what I remember, you *would* understand. Israel is the only nation in the world whose very existence is threatened. Should Israel lose but one war, it would mean her end and ours as well. But I have faith. Faith in the God of Abraham, Isaac, and Jacob, and even in His creation. Without it no action would be possible. And action is the only remedy to indifference, the most insidious danger of all. Isn't this the meaning of Alfred Nobel's legacy? Wasn't his fear of war a shield against war?

There is so much to be done, there is so much that can be done. One person—a Raoul Wallenberg, an Albert Schweitzer, a Martin Luther King, Jr.—one person of integrity can make a difference, a difference of life and death.

As long as one dissident is in prison, our freedom will not be true. As long as one child is hungry, our lives will be filled with anguish and shame. What all these victims need above all is to know that they are not alone; that we are not forgetting them, that when their voices are stifled we shall lend them ours, that while their freedom depends on ours, the quality of our freedom depends on theirs.

This is what I say to the young Jewish boy wondering what I have done with his years. It is in his name that I speak to you and that I express to you my deepest gratitude. No one is as capable of gratitude as one who has emerged from the Kingdom of Night. We know that every moment is a moment of grace, every hour an offering; not to share them would mean to betray them. Our lives no longer belong to us alone; they belong to all those who need us desperately.

Thank you, Chairman Aarvik. Thank you, members of the Nobel Committee. Thank you, people of Norway, for declaring on this singular occasion that our survival has meaning for mankind.

The Nobel Lecture*

ANI MAAMIN, I believe . . . I believe in the coming
of the Messiah . . . I believe in the hope for a future,
just as I believe in the irresistible power of memory.

A Hasidic legend tells us that the great Rabbi
Israel Baal Shem Tov, Master of the Good Name,
also known as the Besht, undertook an urgent and
perilous mission. He wanted to hasten the coming of
the Messiah. The Jewish people, all humanity, were
suffering too much, beset by too many evils. They had
to be saved, and swiftly. For having tried to meddle
with history, the Besht was punished. He was banished
along with his faithful servant to a distant island. In
despair the servant implored his master to exercise his
mysterious powers in order to bring them both home.
"Impossible," the Besht replied. "My powers, my
mystical powers, have been taken from me."

"Then, please, say a prayer, recite a litany, work
a miracle."

* Delivered on December 11, 1986, in Oslo, Norway.

"Impossible," the Master replied. "I have forgotten everything." And so they fell to weeping.

Suddenly the Master turned to his servant and asked, "My friend, remind me of a prayer, any prayer."

"If only I could," said the servant. "I too have forgotten everything."

"Everything, absolutely everything?"

"Everything," said the servant, "except . . ."

"Except what?"

"Except the alphabet!"

At that the Besht cried out joyfully, "Then what are you waiting for? Begin reciting the alphabet, and I shall repeat after you." And together the two exiled men began to recite, at first in whispers, then more loudly, the Hebrew equivalent to the ABCs: "*Aleph bet gimmel,*" and over again, "*Aleph bet gimmel,*" and each time more vigorously, more fervently, until the Besht ultimately regained his memory and thus his powers.

I love this story, for I love stories; but I especially love this one for it illustrates the messianic exhortation and expectation which remains my own. It also illustrates the importance of friendship to man's ability to transcend his condition. I love it most of all because it emphasizes the mystical power of memory. Without memory, our existence would be barren and opaque, like a prison cell into which no light penetrates, like a tomb which rejects the living. Memory served and saved the Besht, and if anything can, it is memory that will save humanity. For me, hope without memory is like memory without hope.

Just as man cannot live without dreams, man cannot live without expectations. If dreams reflect the past, hope summons the future. Does this mean that our future can be built on a rejection of the past? Surely such a choice is not necessary. The two are not incompatible. The opposite of the past is not the future but the absence of future; the opposite of the future is not the past but the absence of past. The loss of one is equivalent to the sacrifice of the other.

A recollection. The time: after the war. The place: Paris. A young man, a young Jew, struggles to readjust to life. His mother, his father, his small sister are gone. He is alone—on the verge of despair. And yet he does not give up. On the contrary, this young Jew strives to find a place among the living. He acquires a new language. He makes a few friends who, like himself, believe that the memory of evil will serve as a shield against evil, that the memory of death will serve as a shield against death. This he must believe. It is a kind of existential belief—like Kierkegaard, he *must* believe in it in order to go on. For he has just returned from a universe where God, betrayed by His creatures, covered His face in order not to see. Mankind, jewel of His creation, had succeeded in building an inverted Tower of Babel, reaching not toward heaven but toward an anti-heaven, and there to create a parallel society, a new "creation" with its own princes and gods, laws and principles, jailers and prisoners. A world where the past no longer counted—no longer meant anything.

Stripped of possessions, all human ties severed, the prisoners found themselves in a social and cultural void. "Forget," they were told. "Forget where you came from; forget who you were. Only the present matters." But the present was only a blink of God's eye. The slaughterer himself was godlike, almighty; it was he who decided who would live and who would die, who would be tortured and who would be rewarded. Night after night, seemingly endless processions vanished into the flames, lighting up the sky. Fear dominated the universe. Indeed, this was another universe; the very laws of nature had been transformed. Children looked like old men, old men whimpered like children. Men and women from every corner of Europe were suddenly reduced to nameless and faceless creatures, desperate for the same ration of bread or soup, dreading the same end. Even their silence was the same, for it resounded with the memory of those who were gone. Life in this accursed universe was so distorted, so unnatural that a new species evolved. Waking among the dead, one wondered if one were still alive.

And yet some of us remember that real despair did not seize us until later, until after the war. Psychiatrists refer to this as "latency." We need a certain period between the event and the response to the

event, because the immediate response would be overwhelming, tragic; and inevitably the person going
through the experience would be crushed by it. We
needed time to rethink and reevaluate our acquired
certainties.

As we emerged from the nightmare and began to
search for meaning, all those lovers of art and poetry,
of Bach and Goethe, who coldly and deliberately ordered the massacres and participated in them, what
did their metamorphosis signify? Could anything explain their loss of ethical, cultural, and religious memory? How could we ever understand the passivity of
the onlookers and, yes, the silence of the Allies?

To this day, I don't understand how the enemy
drove ten thousand Jews to Babi Yar day after day
between Rosh Hashanah (the New Year) and Yom
Kippur (the Day of Atonement). Babi Yar is not
outside Kiev, Babi Yar is *in* Kiev—and they were all
machine-gunned. They went through the streets, people saw them marching, heard the machine guns.
What happened to the people? Did they become deaf,
blind, mute? I cannot understand their indifference.
Nor can I understand, and I say so with pain in my
heart, the silence of people who were good people.
Roosevelt was a good man and Churchill was a great
man. They had the courage then to fight the mighty
Hitler and his powerful armies. But when it came to
saving Jews, somehow the principles of humanity no
longer applied. What happened? What made Roose-

velt a different person? I do not understand it. And to me, a Jew who comes from a deeply religious background, there was the question of questions: *Where was God in all this?* It seemed as impossible to conceive of Auschwitz with God as to conceive of Auschwitz without God. The tragedy of the believer is much greater than the tragedy of the nonbeliever. But after the war, whether one was a believer or not, everything had to be reassessed because everything had changed. With one stroke, mankind's achievements seemed to have been erased.

Was Auschwitz a consequence of "civilization" or was it an aberration? All we know is that Auschwitz called that civilization into question as it called into question everything that had preceded Auschwitz. Scientific abstraction, social and economic contention, nationalism, xenophobia, religious fanaticism, racism, mass hysteria, and, of course, anti-Semitism, both religious and social—all found their ultimate expression in Auschwitz.

The next question my generation had to face was: Why go on? If memory continually brought us back to the altar of death, why build a home? Why go to school? Why reach out to others? Why make friends? Why trust? Why have faith in anyone or in yourself? How can I be sure that tomorrow the sun will shine when night seems eternal? And why bring children into a world in which God and man betrayed their trust in each other?

And yet, it is surely human to forget, even to want to forget. The ancients saw it as a divine gift. Indeed, if memory helps us to survive, forgetting helps us to go on living. How can we go on with our daily lives if we remain constantly aware of the dangers and ghosts surrounding us? The Talmud even tells us that without the ability to forget, man would soon cease to learn. Without the ability to forget, man would live in a permanent, paralyzing fear of death. Only God and God alone can and must remember everything all the time.

How are we to reconcile our supreme duty toward memory with the need to forget that is essential to life? No generation has had to confront this paradox with such urgency. The survivors wanted to communicate everything to the living: the victims' solitude and sorrow, their tears, their despair, their madness, the prayers of the doomed beneath a fiery sky. They needed to tell of the beggar who, in a sealed cattle car, began to sing as an offering to his companions, and of the little girl who, hugging her grandmother, whispered, "Grandmother, don't be afraid, don't be sorry to die— I'm not. It's not worth going on living."

Each one of us felt compelled to recall every story, every encounter. Each one of us felt compelled to bear witness. Such were the wishes of the dying, the testament of the dead. Since the so-called civilized world had no use for their lives, then let it be inhabited by their deaths.

The great Jewish historian Shimon Dubov served as our guide and inspiration. Until the moment of his death he said over and over again in Yiddish to his companions in the Riga ghetto, "*Yidden, shreibt un fershreibt!*" ("Jews, write it all down!") His words were heeded. Overnight, countless victims became chroniclers and historians in the ghettos, even in the death camps. Even members of the *Sonderkommando*, those inmates forced to burn their fellow inmates' corpses before being burned in turn, left behind extraordinary documents. To testify became an obsession. They left us poems and letters, prayers, diaries, fragments of testimony, some known throughout the world, others that should be published but remain unpublished.

After the war we reassured ourselves that it would be enough to relate a single night in Auschwitz, to tell of the cruelty, the senselessness of murder, and the outrage born of apathy; it would be enough to find the right word and the propitious moment to say it, to shake humanity out of its indifference and keep the torturer from torturing ever again. We thought it would be enough to read the world a poem written by a child in the Theresienstadt ghetto to ensure that no child anywhere would ever again have to endure hunger or fear of solitude. It would be enough to describe a death camp "selection" to prevent the human right to dignity from being violated ever again.

We thought it would be enough to tell of the

tidal wave of hatred which broke over the Jewish people for men everywhere to decide once and for all to
put an end to hatred of anyone who is "different"—
whether black or white, Jew or Arab, Christian or
Moslem—anyone whose orientation differs politically,
philosophically, sexually. A naive undertaking? Of
course. But not without a certain logic.

We tried. It was not easy. At first, because of the
language: language failed us. We would have to invent a new vocabulary, for our own words were inadequate, anemic.

And then, too, the people around us refused to
listen; and even those who listened refused to believe;
and even those who believed could not comprehend.
Of course they could not. Nobody could. The experience of the camps defies comprehension. Can you
understand, can anyone understand how a nation of
such culture, of such power, could all of a sudden invent death camps, death factories, and mobilize its
entire industry, its science, its philosophy, its passion,
to kill Jewish people? For what? I cannot understand;
even from *their* viewpoint it was madness. In 1944,
when they were losing the war, they gave priority to
trains leading Jews to their deaths over military trains
bringing soldiers and weapons to the front. That
doesn't make sense. But it was going on to the very
last day. Wouldn't the story of their irrational criminal
behavior prevent irrational crimes against humanity
elsewhere?

So we tried. Perhaps if we were to tell the tale things would change. Have we failed? I often think we have. If someone had told us in 1945 that in our lifetime religious wars would rage on virtually every continent, that thousands of children would once again be dying of starvation, we would not have believed it. Or that racism and fanaticism would flourish once again. Nor would we have believed there would be governments that would deprive men and women of their basic rights merely because they dare to dissent. Governments of the Right and of the Left still subject those who dissent—writers, scientists, intellectuals—to torture and persecution. How is one to explain all this unless we consider the defeat of memory?

How is one to explain any of it? The outrage of apartheid which continues unabated? Racism in itself is dreadful, but when it pretends to be legal, and therefore just, it becomes even more repugnant. Without comparing apartheid to Nazism and to its Final Solution—for that defies all comparison—one cannot help but assign the two systems, in their supposed legality, to the same camp. What about the outrage of terrorism? Of the hostages in Iran, the cold-blooded massacre in the synagogues in Istanbul, Paris, and Vienna, the senseless deaths in the streets of Beirut?

Terrorism must be outlawed by all civilized nations—not explained or rationalized, but fought and eradicated. Nothing can, nothing will, justify the murder of innocent people and helpless children . . . and the outrage of preventing men and women, marvelous men and women like Andrei Sakharov, Vladimir and Masha Slepak, Ida Nudel, Josef Begun, Victor Brailowski, Zakhar Zonshein, Juli Edelstein, and all the others, known and unknown, from leaving their country.

Yesterday afternoon, when I left this hall with its overwhelming emotional aspect, my wife and I went to our hotel and began calling *refuseniks* in the Soviet Union. That is what we did all afternoon. We wanted them to know that, especially on this day, we were thinking not only of our joy but also of their plight. We went on calling them, one after the other. At one point they began calling back. The whole afternoon was a dialogue of human solidarity. If ever your prize had concrete, immediate meaning, distinguished Members of the Committee, it was yesterday afternoon: to those Jews in Russia it meant that here in this place we care, we think of them, and we shall never forget.

As a Jew, I must also speak about Israel. After two thousand years of exile and thirty-eight years of sovereignty, Israel still does not enjoy peace. I would like to see the people of Israel, my people, establish the foundation for a constructive relationship with all its Arab neighbors, as it has done with Egypt. We must see to it that the Jewish people in Israel and all people in the Middle East enjoy some measure of peace and hope . . . at last. We must exert pressure on all those in power to come to terms.

And here we come back to memory. We must

remember the suffering of my people, as we must remember that of the Ethiopians, the Cambodians, the
boat people, the Palestinians, the Miskito Indians, the
Argentinian *desaparecidos*—the list seems endless.

Let us remember Job, who, having lost everything—his children, his friends, his possessions, and
even his argument with God—still found the strength
to begin again, to rebuild his life. Job was determined
not to repudiate the creation, however imperfect, that
God had entrusted to him.

Job, our ancestor. Job, our contemporary. Everything in our tradition tells us that Job was not a Jew,
but his suffering concerns us. It concerns us so much
that we have taken his language into our liturgy. His
ordeal concerns all humanity. Did he ever lose his
faith? If so, he rediscovered it within his rebellion. He
demonstrated that faith is essentially a rebellion, and
that hope is possible beyond despair, but not without
ignoring despair. The source of his hope was memory,
as it must be ours. Because I remember, I despair.
Because I remember, I have the duty to reject despair.

I remember the killers and I despair; I remember
the victims, and on their behalf and for their sake and
for their children's sake, I must invent a thousand and
one reasons to hope.

There may be times when we are powerless to
prevent injustice, but there must never be a time when
we fail to protest. The Talmud tells us that by saving a
single human being—and there are two versions: one

version says a single Jewish human being and the other version says any human being—man can save the world. We may be powerless to open all the jails and free all the prisoners, but by declaring our solidarity with one prisoner, we indict all jailers. None of us is in a position to eliminate war, but it is our obligation to denounce it and expose it in all its hideousness. War leaves no victors, only victims.

I began with the story of the Besht. And like the Besht, mankind needs to remember—more than ever. Mankind needs peace more than ever, for our entire planet, threatened by nuclear war, is in danger of total elimination—a destruction, an annihilation only man can provoke, only man can prevent. It is all up to us. The lesson, the only lesson that I have learned from my experiences, is twofold: first, that there are no plausible answers to what we have endured. There are no theological answers, there are no psychological answers, there are no literary answers, there are no philosophical answers, there are no religious answers. The only conceivable answer is a *moral* answer. This means there must be a moral element in whatever we do. Second, that just as despair can be given to me only by another human being, hope too can be given to me only by another human being. Mankind must remember also, and above all, that like hope and whatever hope signifies, peace is not God's gift to his creatures. Peace is a very special gift—it is our gift to each other. And so, *Ani maamin*—I believe—that we must have hope for one another also because of one another. And *Ani maamin*—I believe—that because of our children and their children we should be worthy of that hope, of that redemption, and of some measure of peace.

I thank you.

ACKNOWLEDGMENTS

Several of the essays collected here have appeared separately in other publications: "Why I Write," The New York Times, April 14, 1985 (originally published in Confronting the Holocaust: The Impact of Elie Wiesel, edited by Alvin Rosenfeld and Irving Greenberg, Indiana University Press, 1978), translated by Rosette C. Lamont; "To Believe or Not to Believe," The Jerusalem Post, September 15, 1985, translated from the French by Judy Cooper Weill; "Inside a Library," and "The Stranger in the Bible," published as a pamphlet by the Hebrew Union College–Jewish Institute of Religion, 1980; "A Celebration of Friendship," Through the Sound of Many Voices: Essays in Honor of W. Gunther Plaut, Lester and Orpen Denny's Publishers, Toronto, 1982; "Peretz Markish," The Jewish Frontier, August–September 1981; "Pilgrimage to the Kingdom of Night," The New York Times, November 4, 1979; "Pilgrimage to Sighet," The New York Times, October 14, 1984; "Kaddish in Cambodia," The Jewish Chronicle, April 18, 1980; "Making the Ghosts Speak," The Christian Century, May 27, 1981; "Passover," New York Newsday, April 8, 1984; "Trivializing Memory," The New York Times, June 11, 1989; "Testimony at The Barbie Trial," New York Newsday, June 28, 1987; "What Really Makes Us Free?" Parade Magazine, December 27, 1987; "Are We Afraid of Peace?" Parade Magazine, March 19, 1989.

ABOUT THE AUTHOR

ELIE WIESEL received the Nobel Peace Prize in Oslo, Norway, on December 10, 1986. His Nobel citation reads: "Wiesel is a messenger to mankind. His message is one of peace and atonement and human dignity. The message is in the form of a testimony, repeated and deepened through the works of a great author." He is Andrew Mellon Professor in the Humanities at Boston University and the author of more than thirty books. Mr. Wiesel lives in New York City with his family.